Foregone Conclusions

Contraversions
Critical Studies in Jewish Literature, Culture, and Society
Daniel Boyarin and Chana Kronfeld, General Editors

1. A Radical Jew: Paul and the Politics of Identity, by Daniel Boyarin
2. On the Margins of Modernism: Decentering Literary Dynamics, by Chana Kronfeld
3. The Two Shores of Yabbok: Sickness and Death in Ashkenazy Judaism, by Sylvie-Ann Goldberg, translated by Carol Cosman
4. Foregone Conclusions: Against Apocalyptic History, by Michael André Bernstein

Foregone Conclusions

Against Apocalyptic History

MICHAEL ANDRÉ BERNSTEIN

UNIVERSITY OF CALIFORNIA PRESS

Berkeley   Los Angeles   London

University of California Press
Berkeley and Los Angeles, California

University of California Press, Ltd.
London, England

© 1994 by
The Regents of the University of California

Library of Congress Cataloging-in-Publication Data

Bernstein, Michael André, 1947–
    Foregone conclusions : against apocalyptic history / Michael André
Bernstein.
        p.   cm. — (Contraversions ; 4)
    "A Centennial book."
    Includes bibliographical references and index.
    ISBN 0-520-08785-2
    1. Holocaust, Jewish (1939–1945), in literature.   2. Appelfeld,
Aron. Badenhaim, 'ir nofesh.   3. Victims in literature.
    4. Holocaust, Jewish (1939–1945)—Influence.   5. Jews—History—
Philosophy.   I. Title.   II. Title: Against apocalyptic history.
III. Series.
PN56.H55B47   1994
809'.93358—dc20   93-39502
                                                                                          CIP

for

ROBERT ALTER

*Et nostre liberté volontaire n'a point de production qui soit
plus proprement sienne que celle de l'affection et amitié.*

Contents

Acknowledgments

In many ways, *Foregone Conclusions* is a collaborative venture both in the shaping of its ideas as they now appear and in their gradual unfolding over the time of their composition. Such phrases, as we all know, are the commonplaces of acknowledgments, rhetorical flourishes meaningful only in the carefully limited context in which they are expressed. Here, however, the words designate an indebtedness and recognition of support that extends beyond the common courtesy of the genre. The traditions with which this book deals are the ones out of which I myself have come; the debates that are taken up in these pages are those I have overheard since childhood, and the arguments in which my text now seeks to intervene are, in the deepest sense, family quarrels. In *Per Amica Silentia Lunae*, Yeats says that "we make out of the quarrel with others, rhetoric, but of the quarrel with ourselves, poetry." This is not a volume of poetry, and it hopes to persuade by the logic and discursive reasoning specific to critical prose. Yet it is far from being merely "a quarrel with others." On the contrary, it is a debate with those "others" whose voices I can hear within my own auditory consciousness, who are, in their very differences and polemical opposition, nonetheless part of myself as well.

But this book is also collaborative in a more traditional sense. Several years ago, on our way back from a conference, Gary Saul Morson started to tell me about a new concept for which he had coined the term *sideshadowing*. As he went on to explain what he meant by the word, I interjected that not only did I share his sense that such a term could illuminate a complex range of theoretical problems, but I, too, had been working on a similar configuration of issues. To extend Morson's idea of *sideshadowing*, I coined the complementary term *backshadowing*, and we began to outline a two-part book for which each of us would write a separate section based on our particular concerns. We each composed our sections independently, but they benefited from our frequent conversations and reading of each other's drafts. In the event, our sections became both too long and too disparate in their focuses to make the original idea of a single book feasible. Morson's part, entitled *Narrative and Freedom: The Shadows of Time,* is scheduled to appear in print from Yale University Press virtually simultaneously with the publication of *Foregone Conclusions.* And rather than refer in my endnotes to Morson's study each time a reader might usefully compare our treatment of analogous questions, it is more helpful simply to say that our two books continue, under separate covers, a dialogue that began within a single frame.

My sense of a collaborative enterprise is further sustained by an awareness that, from the outset, this project has benefited from the generous encouragement and steadying advice of a number of friends, colleagues, and students. I am well aware that my argument's claims to contribute to so many seemingly diverse fields will appear as at once contentious and over-reaching. I have tried to think my way through a knot of interlocked questions, in a way that must seem against the grain of much of what we regularly hear and read. But my thinking derives no small measure of its enabling curiosity from the intense involvement of others who have assisted me, and it stands ready, at every turn, to welcome whatever new rectification or guidance other voices can bring. In the meantime, I am very grateful for the chance to express my continuing appreciation for all that my first readers have already given me. To Alex Zwerdling, Thomas G. Rosenmeyer, the late Leo Lowenthal, Lawrence Rainey, and M. E. Brugger, my sincere appreciation for having helped make this book better than it could ever have been without their counsel. I am also glad to acknowledge how much I learned from the energetic discussions with the students in my spring 1993 graduate seminar at Berkeley. Doris Kretschmer and Douglas Abrams Arava of the University of California Press were enthusiastic and helpful from the outset and have my gratitude for their personal commitment to my work. I also want to thank my copy- and project editor, Betsey Scheiner, as well as my designer, Barbara Jellow, for their helpfulness and expertise. My dedicating this book to Robert Alter is an index of how our dialogues have always quickened my sense of the very possibility of this project, and a reminder of the continuing pleasures of a friendship, conducted both on and off the tennis court. My wife, Jeanne Wolff Bernstein, and our daughter, Anna-Nora, are the larger context in which all my dialogues take place and find their rightful proportion.

I want to thank the Guggenheim Foundation, the Koret Foundation, the director and staff of Mishkenot Sha'ananim in Jerusalem, the U.C. Berkeley President's Fellowship in the Humanities, and the Departments of English and Comparative Literature at U.C. Berkeley, for granting me the time and the funds to work on this study.

In very different versions, sections of this book appeared in the following journals: *Raritan, TriQuarterly,* and *Modernism/Modernity.* I am grateful to all the editors involved, both for their valuable suggestions and for permission to reprint portions of these essays here.

For his generous authorization to use the photograph *Almstadtstraße 43: Diaprojektion eines ehemaligen hebräischen Buchladens* on the cover of the book, I would like to thank the artist, Shimon Attie.

1

AGAINST FORESHADOWING

A: What is the great world-historical event of 1875?
B: Vladimir Ilych Lenin turned five!

A characteristic Russian joke
during the Brezhnev era

Early in *The Brothers Karamazov,* we are offered a series of speculations about the paternity of Smerdyakov, born after the rape of an impoverished and feeble-minded orphan, "Stinking Lizaveta." Since Smerdyakov ends up murdering Fyodor Karamazov, the whole narrative and intellectual thrust of the novel depends on Smerdyakov being Fyodor's bastard son. But astonishingly, for a writer so dependent in his political journalism on a cosmos of pre-ordained plots and historical destinies, Dostoevsky, for a brief moment, deliberately allows Smerdyakov's parentage to remain unclear. Suspicion falls on a certain Karp, an escaped convict, and on various other drunken "gentlemen" of the town, until it finally dissolves into the forever undecidable past. Here, in the heavily forestructured universe of *The Brothers Karamazov,* Dostoevsky points to the radical freedom of human beings from any kind of determinism, and his technical, literary way of showing this is to throw into doubt the time-honored device of foreshadowing. Smerdyakov may grow up to be his father's killer— indeed, without that resolution there would be no story to tell—but he is not *predestined* for that deed, and the man he does murder may, in fact, not even have been his biological father. Such a strategy can be defined as a kind of *sideshadowing:* a gesturing to the side, to a present dense with multiple, and mutually exclusive, possibilities for what is to come.[1] In narrative terms, sideshadowing is best understood

1

in opposition to the familiar technique of foreshadowing, a technique whose enactment can vary tremendously in its degree of intri-
cacy, but whose logic must always value the present, not for itself, but
as the harbinger of an already determined future. The Russian joke
quoted above is a fine jibe at the remarkably crude foreshadowing
that habitually characterizes any global and monolithic way of thinking, and it is probably salutary to insist that *all* foreshadowing is vulnerable to the kind of irony that the Russians learned over the decades to direct at their own institutionalized version of the *topos*.

Although we usually think of them as discrete categories, there are
intimate and mutually elucidating similarities in how we make sense
of literary fictions, historical events, and individual biographies.
These similarities are both formal (a book's language and structure)
and ethical (its significance in human terms). Hence, applying the
same analytic scrutiny to historical accounts and literary texts provides a powerful way to understand the underlying principles governing both kinds of writing. And because the kinds of stories we tell
ourselves and one another are a central portion, perhaps even the
core, of who we are and, more technically, because the ways we narrate and order those stories are as significant in their effect as is their
thematic content, the implications of foreshadowing go far beyond
what strictly formalist literary considerations suggest.

At its extreme, foreshadowing implies a closed universe in which
all choices have already been made, in which human free will can
exist only in the paradoxical sense of choosing to accept or willfully—
and vainly—rebelling against what is inevitable. This is the case
whether the foreshadowing takes place at the theological, historical,
or psychological level. Christian apologetics, Marxist teleology, and
psychological determinism are striking instances of how powerful our
impulse toward foreshadowing can be, and make clear how it is
bound to seem arbitrarily colonizing of, and condescending to, any
moments that threaten to exceed its interpretive grasp. Thus, the
Christian Church Fathers' reduction of the Hebrew Bible to a cycle
of prefigurations of and preparations for the Gospel story is, for all
its intellectual dexterity and inventiveness (especially the elaboration
of figural allegory), rightly viewed by Jews as a brutal impoverishment

of the original texts. "Supersessionist" theology necessarily reduces the predecessor text to an "Old Testament," whose independent significance is fundamentally annulled once it is construed as only the first stage of a process culminating in the annunciation of a "new" and more complete truth. Think for a moment of the Pauline Epistle in which the wandering of the Jews in the desert is read as a *figura* of the challenges facing the first Christian communities, or the ways in which the Christian exegetical tradition interpreted the story of Jonah as a prefiguration of the Savior's Passion, with the three days in the belly of the whale foreshadowing the three days when Christ harrowed Hell between the Crucifixion and the Resurrection. In its encounters with the Hebrew Bible, Christian hermeneutics read the central events of Jewish tradition as "witnessing," in the sense of foreshadowing, the authority of its own stories. Hence, for example, the pressure in the Christian tradition to rename a narrative like the Hebrew Bible's *Akedah,* or "Binding," of Isaac as the "Sacrifice" of Isaac, a self-conscious refiguring designed to make the Jewish story interpretable as an anticipation of Christ's sacrifice on the cross.[2] Indeed, there is a strong sense in which the very idea of history as a linear unfolding from darkness toward light, and from ignorance toward truth, is rooted neither in Jewish nor in Classical thinking but, as Jonathan Boyarin has argued, entirely in "the early church fathers' idea of the progression from Judaism to Christianity."[3] And much as the Jewish and pagan world found the claims of the first Christian missionaries incomprehensible, to someone not already persuaded of the truth of their secular revelations, the conventional Marxist explanations of why the working classes stayed so loyal to their national governments at the outbreak of the First World War, or of why large sections of the German proletariat adhered to Nazism, often against their own economic interest, can seem astonishingly dismissive of the peculiarities of each specific circumstance.

Sideshadowing's attention to the unfulfilled or unrealized possibilities of the past is a way of disrupting the affirmations of a triumphalist, unidirectional view of history in which whatever has perished is condemned because it has been found wanting by some irresistible historico-logical dynamic. Against foreshadowing, sideshadowing

champions the incommensurability of the concrete moment and refuses the tyranny of all synthetic master-schemes; it rejects the conviction that a particular code, law, or pattern exists, waiting to be
uncovered beneath the heterogeneity of human existence. Instead
of the global regularities that so many intellectual and spiritual movements claim to reveal, sideshadowing stresses the significance of random, haphazard, and unassimilable contingencies, and instead of the
power of a system to uncover an otherwise unfathomable truth, it
expresses the ever-changing nature of that truth and the absence of
any predictive certainties in human affairs. Or in Robert Musil's more
subtly ironic formulation, what we need to recognize is the reality of
underdetermination, the fact that events do not occur because of any
logical or historical necessity. As Ulrich, Musil's Man Without Qualities, explains with his "Principle of the Insufficient Cause," even the
laws of probability are regularly transgressed by the course of events,
and the unlikely outcome can take place as often as the more plausible one: "You know of course what the principle of the sufficient
cause is. Only, people make an exception where they themselves are
concerned. In real life, by which I mean our personal and also our
public-historical life, what happens is always what has no good
cause."[4]

Because so many of our greatest fictions seem, in the confidence
of their massiveness and sweep, like monuments of inevitability, ef-
fortlessly enfolding each turn of events, each narrative "accident,"
into the larger structure of the whole, many readers have responded
to works like Philip Roth's *The Counterlife* or Borges's *Ficciones* with a
feeling of liberation at the text's playful acceptance of contradictory
possibilities. A sense of readerly delight is often triggered by a work
that self-consciously plays with the certainties of what used to be
called "major form." In one of his working notes to *The Counterlife,*
Roth provides a schematic formula for a novel that will resist any
closure based on models of biographical fixity: "Life can go this way
or life can go that way. The alternative, the alternative to the alternative, etc."[5] Put so starkly, Roth's directive to himself is both a literary commonplace and one of the cornerstones of imaginative creation at least since *Don Quixote.* Particularly in modern literature, the

kind of experimental playfulness that Roth's dictum encourages has been fundamental for an ever-growing canon of technically adroit and epistemologically probing explorations by writers ranging from Georges Perec and Italo Calvino to Vladimir Nabokov and John Ashbery.

And yet it is worth stopping for a moment to register how, quite beyond the challenge posed by contemporary experimental fiction, any account of literary creation that takes the structural coherence of the classical novel as its privileged model is itself already historically blinkered. As soon as the paradigmatic structure for an extended narrative is not limited to the well-wrought novel developed over the past two hundred years, it becomes clear that many of the fundamental storytelling conventions of our culture have never fallen under the sway of a single story unfolding along an irreversible temporal continuum. In *The Marriage of Cadmus and Harmony,* Roberto Calasso gives eloquent voice to this realization: "Mythical figures live many lives, die many deaths, and in this way they differ from the characters we find in novels, who can never go beyond the single gesture. But in each of these lives and deaths all the others are present, and we can hear their echo."[6] Commenting on this passage, Jasper Griffin notes that "the novel, restricted to a single version, makes it more dense, more detailed—to compensate for its lost variants. . . . [But some modern novels] struggle to reclaim that openness, to regain indeterminacy; in the novel such antiquarianism is regarded as experimental, avant-garde. The reader is dizzied by the variants, just as 'the mythographer lives in a permanent state of chronological vertigo.' "[7] But "the single version" of a tale, even the single life lived once and once only, is no longer the unchallengeable narrative assumption of the novel, and works like Yehuda Amichai's *Not of This Time, Not of This Place* (1963), Roth's *The Counterlife* (1986), or Carol Anshaw's *Aquamarine* (1992) seek precisely to include the numerous "lost variants" of their stories within a single book. Yet perhaps, rather than eliciting the kind of dizziness, whether exuberant or irritated, that Griffin describes, the narrative's refusal to stay confined within the hierarchy of a fixed timetable and strict causality, both based on a conception of linear and irreversible historical progression, can be felt as deeply consonant with a layer of self-understanding that more closed narrative forms have been unwilling to engage. Even at the level of an individual's momentary thought rather than entire life, we instinctively recognize the force of the counter-story, the never articulated, but also never discountable, possibilities that any too strictly fixed interpretation risks foreclosing. So, for example, throughout Hermann Broch's *The Sleepwalkers* (1930–32) there is a series of arresting moments when, after someone has been described as having certain ideas, the narrator corrects himself and concludes that, in all likelihood, the character thought nothing of the sort.[8] In literature, especially in novels committed to an intense psychological interrogation of individual characters, an assertion of the form "of course x wasn't really thinking this" is habitually taken to signify "these sentences do not transcribe x's exact sentiments because x couldn't voice them so clearly, but they do embody the essence of what x would have said he thought if he were able to express himself with greater precision and self-awareness." But, more interestingly, the sentence could also give voice to a recognition of the extraordinary diversity and unpredictability of human reactions. In this sense, which, I believe, is precisely what Broch intends, the proposition would mean something like "here is one of the many strands of thought x *might* have entertained, but others are equally plausible in this context."

It is worth stressing how different this idea is, in spite of its apparent kinship, from Freud's concept of "overdetermination." In Freud, overdetermination is "a consequence of the work of condensation" and signifies that "formations," like dreams or symptoms, must be attributed to a plurality of determining factors.[9] For writers like Broch, Musil, or Roth, however, the multiplicity of motivations of a dream, thought, or feeling is not the primary issue; instead, the focus is on the multiplicity of the "formations" themselves. In reading these novels, we become trained not to search for ever more deeply intertwined chains of signification intersecting at the "nodal point" of a single expression, but to recognize that a whole orchestration of complex sentiments and concepts might be occurring, not, as it were, archaeologically *beneath* the surface ones as their foundation, but instead, topographically *alongside of,* and temporally *concurrent with,* the one we notice and upon which our attention and interpretive acumen are focused.[10] Novels like these show us how each counterlife is composed of countless counter-moments, and how each thought takes shape as only one realization amid the counter-thoughts that hover as its sideshadows, multiple alternatives existing in a potential space and ready to be brought, by the quickening of imagination or desire, out of the shadows and into the light of formal expression.

It is important to specify that nothing I have said so far argues for any radical relativism or questions the existence of definable concepts and sentiments. To stress the claims of sideshadowing and counter-lives, far from undermining the authority of the concrete instance, is its most radical guarantor precisely because it insists on the primacy of human freedom. It is between the antithetical but twin reductionisms of teleological determinism and radical undecidability, between, to give as examples two of their recent local names, Marxism and Deconstruction, that the prosaics of sideshadowing positions itself, in principle equally at odds with both of its more widely canvassed counter-models.

With these positions, as in all debates with either dogmatism or relativism, a real dialogue is impossible because, to echo Bakhtin, in dogmatism the only "true" answer is already known in advance, and in a thoroughgoing relativism no answer can have any more significance than does its antithesis. To concentrate on the sideshadowed ideas and events, on what did not happen, does not cast doubt on the historicity of what occurred but views it as one among a range of possibilities, a number of which might, with equal plausibility, have taken place instead. The one that actually was realized, though, exists from then on with all the weight afforded by the singularity of what we might call its event-ness. Only the brightness of an actual event can cast sufficient shadow for sideshadowing to matter, and only the felt force of a life can give impetus to the counterlives that seize the imagination. A prosaics of the quotidian requires a willingness to remain receptive to the voices from the shadows in order to safeguard itself from becoming either a new kind of reductionism or a blind affirmation of whatever has triumphed sufficiently to flourish in the glare of actuality. Counterlives count because they are a constituent element of the lives we have, just as it is often by the shadows the sun casts, not by its direct light, that we can best calibrate where we stand.[11]

To keep the claims of both the event and its unrealized alternatives in mind may be more perplexing as a theoretical formulation than as an ongoing act, and problems that critical habit and grammar often urge us to see cleanly divided are in practice usually vitally, and even messily, intertwined. To show just how crucial is the conjunction of life and counterlife, event and its shadow, requires not so much a global schema as a sequence of careful acts of local scrutiny. An investigation such as mine must be cautious not to force a single, limited horizon on a number of radically different texts, much of whose power stems directly from their seeming incommensurability and from their resistance to any generalizable interpretive formula. The more interesting a work of art is, the more it will evade being treated as merely an instance of a general principle, and a project like this, if it is to avoid arbitrariness, must maintain a constant readiness to adjust the balance between its larger assertions and its local evidence with sufficient tact. Ultimately, it is this readiness itself, the willingness to engage what lies outside the direct field of its own proclaimed aim that, more than anything else, stands as both the test and the practice of sideshadowing.

2
BACKSHADOWING AND APOCALYPTIC HISTORY

The syndrome of the System is one of those super-
ideas, alongside which life itself becomes a detail
unworthy of attention. . . . Only for the sake of a
person's right to a private life is living worth while.
Anatoli Sobchak (mayor of St. Petersburg),
The Road to Power

At some point history becomes like topography:
there is no *why* to it, only a *here* and a *there.*
John Updike, *Memoirs of the
Ford Administration*

Our instinctive gratitude to what frees us from the too strictly plotted,
the too seamlessly coherent story, undoubtedly accounts for much of
our pleasure in experimental fiction. But this responsiveness to the
improvisatory is changed decisively at those moments when contemporary history and literature intersect, when the issue becomes one
of representing an event with whose occurrence we are still attempting to come to terms. Especially in the face of a catastrophe, there is
an urge to surrender to the most extreme foreshadowing imaginable,
thereby resisting sideshadowing altogether. We try to make sense of
a historical disaster by interpreting it, according to the strictest teleological model, as the climax of a bitter trajectory whose inevitable
outcome it must be. This sense of wrenching inevitability, like a tragic
hero's vain efforts to avoid his fate, is the cornerstone not only of
Aristotelian tragedy, but of its most powerful literary descendants
across genres and epochs. Yet a historical cataclysm, no matter how

terrible, is not a tragedy, and to interpret it as one would denature the character of what I earlier called its "event-ness." If genres provide a certain way of understanding the world, as well as a constellation of distinct formal characteristics, and if, according to P. N. Medvedev and the Bakhtinians, "one does not first see a given aspect of reality and then shape it to a given set of conventions [but] instead, sees reality 'with the eyes of the genre,' "[1] then classical tragedy is the genre least open to the claims of sideshadowing, just as the tragic hero's destiny is least amenable to the judgments of a prosaic ethics. When an event is so destructive for a whole people, so hideous in its motivation, enactment, and consequences as was the Shoah, there is an almost irresistible pressure to interpret it as one would a tragedy, to regard it as the simultaneously inconceivable and yet foreordained culmination of the entire brutal history of European anti-Semitism. (Because the word *holocaust* carries with it a penumbra of unwelcome theological implications of a divinely sanctioned sacrifice, I have preferred to use the Hebrew word Shoah throughout this book in referring to the Nazi genocide.)[2]

Irving Howe has argued powerfully against interpreting the Shoah as a tragedy, but for entirely different reasons than the ones at issue here, and it is useful to test the logic of his position in order to clarify my own:

> the death camps and mass exterminations . . . give little space for the tragic. . . . In classical tragedy, man is defeated; in the Holocaust, man is destroyed. In tragedy, man struggles against forces that overwhelm him, struggles against the gods and against his own nature; and the downfall that follows may have an aspect of grandeur. This struggle allows for the possibility of an enlargement of character through the purgation of suffering, which in turn may bring a measure of understanding and a kind of peace. But . . . [most of] the Jews destroyed in the camps . . . died . . . not because they chose at all costs to remain Jews, but because the Nazis chose to believe that being Jewish was an unchangeable, irredeemable condition. They were victims of a destruction that, for many of them, had little or only a fragmentary meaning. . . . All of this does not make their death less terrible; it makes their death more terrible.[3]

Howe's description here seems all too accurate as an account of Jewish agony in the Shoah, but it suggests that a different measure of self-consciousness, a changed relationship to the fact of their murder, would have made the event a tragedy. In opposition to this view, sideshadowing and the prosaic worldview allied with it insist that no historical event, no paradigm of struggle, resistance, and acceptance, can transform the death of countless human beings into a tragedy in the literary sense Howe invokes. Tragedy is an arranged genre, and real events do not happen as part of an already narrated form. At most, one might say that in the retelling of individual deaths, in the movement from the complexities of their daily existence into the terrible simplification of their legends, the fate of a small group of individuals united by a common aim, like the Warsaw Ghetto fighters, may give birth, in Yeats's talismanic phrase, to a "terrible beauty."

Tragedy, that is, does not inhere in the actions themselves, not even if those actions are undertaken with the knowledge that they will end in a freely (and hence "heroically") chosen death. Rather, tragedy is created by the ways in which that choice is represented, refigured, and recounted to others. The tragic is a mode of comprehending and giving form to events as a narrative; it is not a mode of existence as such, as we instinctively make clear by labeling as melodramatic someone who attempts to interpret the quotidian details of his own life in a tragic register.

But at the extreme distance from any self-indulgence, even when death is chosen as the certain outcome of a desperate resistance against overwhelming forces, it is not just the courage of the deed, but also its posthumous significance in the communal memory that qualifies it as tragic. Thus, the fighters of the Warsaw Ghetto uprising, or of the Sobibor and Birkenau revolts, have become crucial in the post-war Jewish, and, more particularly, in the Israeli imagination, as proof of a new Jewish readiness to strike back against their oppressors. By *choosing*, rather than helplessly *undergoing* their dying, the resisters can be figured as embodiments of the rebirth of armed Jewish daring and their story can be commemorated as a mixture of heroic and tragic drama.[4] (The museum / study center in Jerusalem,

Yad va-Shem [Monument and Memorial], is explicitly dedicated as much to the Jewish resistance fighters as to the victims of the Shoah.) Like the plot of a classical tragedy, the uprisings against the Nazis took place in a restricted space and time, and the fighters seem tragically heroic to us because we know how they perished and thus we can grasp the beginning and end of each uprising as a single event, fixed in a clear progression of linked episodes. But while it was actually happening, it was experienced instant by instant and person by person, each with different motives and inspirations for fighting, and each with differently formulated explanations of his own involvement. The Shoah as a whole, moreover, can never be represented plausibly as a tragedy because the killings happened as part of an ongoing political and bureaucratic process. In the domain of history, unlike in the world "seen with the eyes of the [tragic] genre," there are always multiple paths and sideshadows, always moment-by-moment events, each of which is potentially significant in determining an individual's life, and each of which is a conjunction, unplottable and unpredictable in advance of its occurrence, of specific choices and accidents. Indeed, every survivor's narrative I have read emphasizes the multiple contingencies, the intersection of fortuitous events too wildly improbable for any fiction, that made survival possible. Primo Levi's account, *Se questo è un uomo,* is, of course, the classic instance of such a survivor's narrative, stressing, as it does, how many separate and unforeseeable incidents had to combine for Levi to live through his time in Auschwitz. These strictly "accidental" occurrences ranged from his encounter with Lorenzo, an Italian civilian worker, who for six months brought the starving captive enough extra food to keep him alive, to the scarlet fever that kept Levi in the infirmary when the Nazis abandoned the camp and took all the able-bodied prisoners with them on a forced march back to Germany, in the course of which virtually every one of them was murdered. Levi makes clear how much pure luck, as well as a gift for improvisation, and a certain inner resilience of character, spirit, and physical health, were necessary to have any chance of survival at all, but for millions of victims of the Shoah none of these qualities was sufficient to preserve them in the death factories: "If the drowned have no story, and single and broad is the path to perdition, the paths to salvation are many, difficult and improbable."[5]

But whether the interpretive model is tragic or historically determinist, the reward of fitting even catastrophic events into a coherent global schema is the pleasure of comprehension, the satisfaction of the human urge to make sense out of every occurrence, no matter how terrible. The simultaneously intellectual and emotional value of understanding the place of a particular event in the most inclusive possible framework is a crucial, and often underestimated, source of "contentment." (It may even be that this pleasure, rather than any direct Aristotelian "catharsis," makes the experience of a tragic worldview so paradoxically gratifying.) Yet every interpretation of the Shoah that is grounded in a sense of historical inevitability resonates with both implicit and often explicit ideological implications, not so much about the world of the perpetrators of the genocide, or about those bystanders who did so little to halt the mass murder, but about the lives of the victims themselves. The bitterness of inevitability, whether seen as tragic or pathetic, endows an event with a meaning, one that can be used both to make an ideationally "rich" sense of the horror and to begin a process of coming to terms with the pain by enfolding it within some larger pattern of signification. And for the Shoah, especially in its uncannily delayed representation in Zionist writing, that pattern has been primarily one of proving the untenability of the Diaspora, and the self-destructive absurdity of the attempts by European and, more specifically, by Austro-German Jewry to assimilate to a society that only waited for its chance to exterminate them.[6] In a recent study, James Young perceptively analyzes "the central negative place of the Holocaust in Zionist ideology as the ultimate consequence of Jewish vulnerability in the Diaspora." In Israel, the Shoah can function as "proof of the untenability of life in exile," and thus can be represented as crystallizing a positive lesson in its very devastation, since what the Nazi killings marked was "not so much the end of Jewish life as . . . the end of viable life in exile."[7] It is with the force of this interpretation, its almost irresistible conclusiveness as a historical and ideological analysis, that I contend throughout much of this book. To have chosen to confront the claims of sideshadowing with the enormity of the Shoah is to test it against a seemingly intractable counter-instance, on the principle that if the validity of sideshadowing can be discerned here, where it seems so difficult to recognize, then its pertinence in cases that are not as morally and theoretically arduous will be more readily apparent. The logic involved is only a particularly sharp instantiation of the medieval guideline that a single, powerful lesson is more instructive than a host of minor ones (*Exemplum docet, exempla obscurant*). If the Shoah is so critical a test case, it is precisely because it is also the one in which so much is at stake, humanly as well as epistemologically, in the simultaneously impossible and unavoidable debate about its meaning. At the same time, it is important to emphasize that I am not claiming that the enormity of the Shoah makes the consideration of more quotidian historical events superfluous. Rather, narratives about the Shoah can serve as exemplary test cases for my position both because of the importance of the Shoah for modern consciousness and because it has so often been represented through a plot governed by a logic of historical inevitability. Such emplotment either explicitly or implicitly rejects the relevance of sideshadowing, and hence provides the kind of totalizing master narrative against which the counterhistory proposed here can be heard most effectively.

But even to speak about a "debate" in this context is potentially misleading. It may suggest, quite wrongly, that the issue is one of the "textuality" (and hence the deconstructibility) of historical events. Although it is obviously the case that our knowledge of the Shoah, as of all events at which we were not actually present, depends on the record of others, written, spoken, filmed, or preserved in a myriad of man-made artifacts, a knowledge so mediated does not therefore cease to be knowledge. The Shoah can stand as a kind of limit case exposing the moral bankruptcy of a theoretical project in which the event-ness of the past is denied its unique specificity and force. Rather than casting doubt on the event-ness of history, sideshadowing helps us to reckon the human cost of an occurrence by reminding us of all that its coming-into-existence made impossible. The nonlives of the sideshadowed events that never happened are a part of the emotional/intellectual legacy and aura of each actually occurring event,[8] inflecting it in distinct ways, as, for example, the extinction of the culture that sustained Yiddish as a spoken and literary language has profoundly changed the way in which Jewish life has been represented since 1945. As Berel Lang rightly insists, "the immediate horror of the death camps has made it difficult to conjure the lives that might have been in lieu of the deaths that were—but this, too, obviously constitutes the actual and continuing loss."[9] Lawrence L. Langer quotes a concentration camp survivor, Philp K., who, in addition to the terrible suffering he both witnessed and endured, is haunted by precisely this loss of all the potential futures that were exterminated in the Shoah: "We'll never recover what was lost. We can't even assess what was lost. Who knows what beauty and grandeur six million could have contributed to the world? Who can measure it up? What standard do you use? How do you count it? How do you estimate it?"[10] I think that some conception of sideshadowing is already intuitively present whenever we talk about the extent of the horror inflicted by the Nazis; indeed, without such a concept, part of the devastation wrought by the Shoah would be permanently blocked from consciousness. Yet while there is nothing controversial about formally describing the workings of sideshadowing in this context, entailed in that account are a number of further implications that directly contest many of the most common narrative practices and theoretical premises flourishing today.

It is essential to recognize here that whenever our sense of what the Shoah destroyed includes, along with their actual deaths, the potential achievements and never realized futures of the children who were murdered, we are already engaged in sideshadowing. The logic of historical inevitability, on the other hand, explicitly suggests that the murdered children were already doomed to perish in the Shoah the instant they were born, hence it would be inconsistent to mourn the adult lives they never experienced or the accomplishments they never attained. Yet a genuine grief for this loss is voiced in books on the genocide that rely on premises of historical inevitability and exploit the narrative techniques of foreshadowing. This constitutes just one of what we will soon see is a whole network of major contradictions in writings about the Shoah, because *only* a rejection of inevitability creates the context in which mourning the obliterated futures of the murdered infants makes any coherent sense.

The realization that we ourselves are often still deeply implicated in historical conflicts and debates whose terms we have not so much shaped as inherited, leads to the most pervasive, but also the most pernicious, variant of foreshadowing, a variant that I have called "backshadowing." Backshadowing is a kind of retroactive foreshadowing in which the shared knowledge of the outcome of a series of events by narrator and listener is used to judge the participants in those events *as though they too should have known what was to come.* Thus, our knowledge of the Shoah is used to condemn the "blindness" and "self-deception" of Austro-German Jewry for their unwillingness to save themselves from a doom that supposedly was clear to see. Backshadowing of this kind, and the presumptions it nourishes, run unchecked, and too often uncriticized, throughout histories, biographies, and novels focusing on the life of Austro-German Jewry, until, in Michael Ignatieff's powerful description, "just as the cultural achievement of the empire is overshadowed by the empire's collapse, so the achievement of Jewish emancipation within the empire is overshadowed by its infamous finale. . . . In no field of historical study does one wish more fervently that historians could write history blind to the future."[11]

But the dilemma cannot be solved by consciously "blinding" ourselves to the future in our histories, if only because it is not at all clear how we either can or should try to bracket all knowledge of the Shoah when we write about the community that perished in it. The discretion required, a discretion that sideshadowing is particularly concerned to teach us, is (1) not to see the future as pre-ordained; and, as a direct corollary, (2) not to use our knowledge of the future as a means of judging the decisions of those living before that (still only possible) future became actual event. Insofar as we are dealing primarily with written documents, the problematics of textuality here have nothing to do with an *aporia* of undecidability and everything to do with the demands of decorum in its full classical sense: the difficult attempt to work out which modes and techniques of representation are appropriately responsive to the exigencies of different human experiences. The two linked forms of discretion I have specified seem, as is so often the case with questions of sideshadowing, uncontroversial enough as general principles, yet in practice they have scarcely ever been heeded in narratives about the Shoah. Thus, to return to Ignatieff's critique of histories of Austro-German Jewry, "because we know that the path for Vienna's Jews led to Mauthausen and Theresienstadt concentration camps, it is easy to be ironic at the expense of those Jews who believed in assimilation into a milieu that was to expel them so brutally. . . . [But to do so is to] evaluate the victims by the degree of prescience with which they anticipate their victimhood . . . and add to the heavy burden of Jewish messianic destiny, the absurd requirement that they be more prescient than other peoples."[12] Such a requirement is precisely what marks numerous accounts about the victims of the Shoah, without their authors seeing that it drains all meaningful reality (that is, a reality made up of specific choices and decisions) from the lives of the people being described. In place of this reality, such accounts substitute an often intolerable, even if unintended, superiority shared by author and reader over the heads, as it were, of the book's subjects.

As a concentrated instance of what I have thus far defined in more general terms, consider the following sentences from a recent and much-praised biography of Franz Kafka. After mentioning the birth of Kafka's sister Elli, on September 15, 1889, the biographer, Ernst Pawel, writes: "Earlier that year, in the not too distant Austrian town of Braunau, one Clara née Plözl, wife of the customs inspector Aloïs Hitler, had given birth to another of the emperor's subjects, a sickly infant whose survival seemed doubtful. He survived."[13] Mentioning the son born to a Braunau customs inspector called Hitler can only elicit the kind of tawdry *frisson* Pawel is trying to achieve if we let ourselves be susceptible to an egregiously blatant act of backshadowing. In 1889 no connection existed yet between the Kafka and Hitler families, and to gesture backward from the terrible years when such a connection, in the form of murderer and victim, did come to occur, is so shamelessly manipulative that it would be easy to laugh away, except that one finds it as a crucial topos in innumerable other texts

on the same theme. Pawel's biography is dense with similarly embarrassing moments, such as the description of Kafka's bar mitzvah: "under Jewish law, Amschel, alias Franz Kafka, became a man on the
morning of June 13, 1896 at the Zigeunersynagoge—the Gypsy Syn-
agogue, so called because of its location on a street formerly known
as Zigeunerstrasse, though the strange name contains a chilling hint
of things to come; a few decades later, the gypsies were to share the
fate of the Jews."[14] Toward the end of the biography, as Kafka is
approaching his early death, Pawel writes, "the family doctor urgently
advised another extended rest, and Kafka, *faute de mieux,* settled on
a boardinghouse in the Bohemian mountain village of Schelesen,
now Zelizy, not far from what was to become the infamous Terezin
concentration camp, through which all three of his sisters passed on
their way to the gas chambers."[15]

These descents into what one may call a kind of Hitler-kitsch[16] are
especially alarming because reviewers of the book proved themselves
so responsive to exactly this strain in Pawel's writing.[17] More unsettling still, many of his tropes surface elsewhere in different hands and
genres. Thus, in a study by the political scientist George S. Berkeley,
Vienna and Its Jews: The Tragedy of Success, it is startling to come across
the following sentence right after a mention of the famous suicide/
murder of the Habsburg crown prince Rudolf and his lover Mary
Vetsera at Mayerling in January 1889: "The other event of special
significance to the Vienna Jews which occurred in 1889 passed unremarked by almost everyone, Jew and Gentile alike. Three months
after Rudolph's death, in the border village of Braunau, a son was
born to Aloïs and Klara Hitler."[18] It is worth lingering for a moment
on the astonishing phrase, "unremarked by almost everyone," with
its surely unintended and risible hint that someone actually did notice the event—perhaps three wise men mysteriously alerted to the
daemonic nativity in Braunau by a kind of negative illumination—
but the coincidence of imagination and phrasing in the Pawel and
Berkeley books requires more than merely being noticed and dismissed. Of course the similarity is not due to plagiarism of any sort;
rather, it is due to the fascination with Hitler that so strongly mobi-
lizes both writers' fantasies. Arthur Danto, in a wonderfully apposite

jest against predestination and foreshadowing, once quipped, "No one came to Mme. Diderot and said, 'Unto you an encyclopaedist is born.' "[19] Danto's irony works so economically because the notion it reduces to absurdity is one to which almost no one would subscribe in the first place. But it is just as true that no one came to Frau Hitler in Braunau and said, "Unto you the Führer is born." Both the quotations by Pawel and Berkeley rely for their force on just such a premise.

If we laugh at the example of Mme. Diderot and yet are capable of responding with a shudder to the portentous news of Hitler's birth without seeing its absurdity, it can only be that in the face of evil on as great a scale as Hitler embodies, there is a general freezing up of normal intellectual discriminations. Yet exactly these moments of confrontation with the monstrous require more, not less, clarity, and demand a greater measure, rather than an abdication, of the ability to stay focused on fundamental distinctions. One of the disturbing "pleasures" apparent in numerous recent fictional representations of Hitler (works as different in their structure and rhetoric as, for example, a film like Hans Jürgen Syberberg's *Hitler: Ein Film aus Deutschland* and a prose fantasy like George Steiner's *The Portage to St. Cristobal of A.H.*) is the way their narratives derive their energy from— and hence transport their audience to—an emotional register whose intensity supposedly places it beyond moral discriminations. In *Crime and Punishment,* Dostoevsky anatomized the feverish excitement that arises when abandoning oneself to the contemplation of horror is confused with authentic imaginative freedom, and a kind of lumpen Raskolnikovism is discernible in what has become a flourishing "Hitler industry." As Alan Mintz has warned, "the fascination with evil is a highly appetitive faculty,"[20] and there is a demoralizing sense in which rhetorics like Pawel's and Berkeley's feed exactly this most dubious of urges. Such a fascination, as much as the logic and ethics of backshadowing, is one of the decisive problems facing anyone who decides to write about the Shoah, and in the next section I specify some of the strategies by which writers hope to short-circuit an "appetitive," and potentially sadomasochistic, immersion in the details of the Nazi barbarity.

The vulgarity of Pawel's and Berkeley's topos of the macabre anti-nativity of Braunau should not obscure how widespread backshadowing is in the great majority of texts about the period. Thus, when Pawel says of Kafka's story, "The Penal Colony," that "the figure of the head torturer himself is a prescient portrait of Adolf Eichmann, drawn from life,"[21] it is no different (except for the spurious specificity of Eichmann, rather than any other Nazi bureaucrat-executioner) from George Steiner's declaration in *Language and Silence* that Kafka had predicted Buchenwald (an analogous example of the kind of false specificity such rhetoric seems to require) and that he had "prophesied the actual forms of that disaster of Western humanism [the Shoah]."[22] Frederick Karl, in a more recent biography, unencouragingly titled *Franz Kafka: Representative Man,* continues the tradition of Kafka-as-prophet-of-Nazism by assimilating the transformation of Gregor Samsa to the image of the Jew in Nazi demonology.[23] Although Karl is forced to admit that "the Samsas do not seem to be Jewish," he hopes that "their vague similarity to the Kafkas gives them some Jewish identity," and, in a still more implausible move to buttress his argument, points out that "Hitler used the term *Ungeziefer* to designate what he considered the vermin of Europe . . . the very word Kafka used in 'The Metamorphosis' to indicate Gregor's new shape."[24] Then, as though a dubious thematic link were not enough, Karl soon enriches it with an even more unilluminating biographical link: "Kafka suffered the kind of privation, desperation, and discontent in Berlin that made possible Hitler's attempt in Munich, in November, to seize power through a *Putsch.* . . . As Kafka wrote 'The Burrow,' about hiding from enemies, the enemy was as close as Munich, planning to flush out moles like Kafka."[25]

There is a host of ill-conceived assumptions in the whole range of apocalyptic/prophetic rhetoric that has become a staple of recent Kafka criticism, as though this kind of belated ennoblement were being offered to compensate for the initial underestimation of the importance of Jewish themes in his writing. It is probably unwise to inflict on even the greatest of writers the obligation of prophecy, and there is little evidence that doing so to Franz Kafka has done much to deepen the quality of responses to his books.[26] Even Gershom

Scholem and Walter Benjamin, for whom Kafka was so vital an imaginative authority, did not attribute the gift of historical prophecy to him.[27] Nor am I really convinced that the critics who do employ such terms mean them in quite the way their sentences declare. Instead, I think that it is actually the critics themselves who, encountering Kafka in the aftermath of the Shoah, have become prophets-after-the-fact and have found themselves unable to read stories like "The Penal Colony" without thinking of the concentration camps. But because of a lingering suspicion that something is seriously awry about interpreting a fictional text in this way, they have retroactively made Kafka into a prophet foreseeing the bestiality that they, not he, know occurred. (Interpreting a prophet is also a distinctly more glamorous activity than commenting on a fiction writer, and no doubt this hierarchic distinction is not without its own efficacy.)

Although the theoretical critique of backshadowing finds a kind of negative aesthetic confirmation from the embarrassing formulations that result when writers rely on it (e.g., the daemonic nativity at Braunau), there exists at least one powerful counter-claim that needs to be confronted because it directly questions the core of my argument. From the Zionist interpretation, Austro-German Jewry had no real future or choices except to leave Europe for *Eretz Israel* or face increasingly severe persecution. (The term *Eretz Israel* signifies "The Land of Israel" and was used through the centuries to designate the Biblical homeland even when there was no prospect of a new Jewish state or political program of returning there.) Of course, even the most pessimistic spokesmen of the Zionist movement never predicted anything as cataclysmic as the Shoah, but at least as early as Herzl, there was no shortage of grim predictions about the fate awaiting the Jews who continued to trust in the civil institutions and legal protection of their native countries. (Vladimir Jabotinski, the founder of Revisionist Zionism, formulated the most intransigent version of this position: "Liquidate the *Galut* [the Diaspora] or the *Galut* will liquidate you.") Hence, in Zionist writing the question of backshadowing is more complicated simply because the dire predictions were made well before the event; thus, at least at the most basic level, Zionist narratives of pre-Nazi European Jewish existence, whether

written before or after 1945, cannot be charged with the same kind
of blatant backshadowing prominent in a Pawel or Berkeley.

However, it is also the case that with the Shoah, if anywhere, the
rule that a sufficient change in quantity amounts to a change in quality seems uncontestable. Zionist predictions never encompassed anything as dreadful as the Shoah, because before it took place, and even
while it was happening, it was simply unimaginable for everyone except its perpetrators. And even they, it is worth remembering, initially
never conceived of being able to enact their anti-Semitism on such a
scale. In *Mein Kampf,* for example, Hitler writes about killing "twelve
or fifteen thousand of these Hebrew corrupters of the people . . .
[by] poison gas."[28] That a demagogue who uttered such sentiments
could have been invited to become Chancellor of Weimar Germany
is rightly felt as appalling, but it is instructive to measure the difference in scale between what Hitler fantasized as possible when writing
his book in 1924 and what the Nazis were able to accomplish once
they had attained state power.

In fact, Zionist attitudes about the values and culture of European
Jewry were always changing as part of the evolving self-definition of
the movement and in response to new outside circumstances and
pressures. For all the grimness of Zionist diagnoses about the dangers
of assimilation, many modifications of even their own forecasts were
required in order to fit the Shoah into the interpretive framework
they had carefully elaborated.[29] As the Israeli social historian Jacob
Katz points out, "anyone who lived through the period of the Holocaust . . . will readily testify that information concerning the Nazi
murder of the Jews, when it first came out, seemed absolutely unbelievable—impossible. In retrospect, however, we tend to conceive of
it as the culmination of a predetermined and unavoidable march of
destiny. . . . in the case of the Holocaust the contradiction is an especially flagrant one because the contradictory attitudes are so em-
phatic."[30] But "still," as Katz goes on to write, "the antinomy persists
between the feeling of having been taken by surprise by the events
of the Holocaust when they occurred and the inclination, after the
fact, to reconstruct those events in such a way as to make them inevitable."[31]

To summarize and extend my argument thus far as succinctly as possible, in the corpus of works on the Shoah, I think there is a powerful but largely unrecognized connection that links together a set of contradictions which are so persistent that they have become constitutive of the whole discourse. On a historical level, there is the contradiction between conceiving of the Shoah as simultaneously un-imaginable *and* inevitable. On an ethical level, the contradiction is between saying no one could have foreseen the triumph of genocidal anti-Semitism, while also claiming that those who stayed in Europe are in part responsible for their fate because they failed to anticipate the danger. On a narrative level, the contradiction is between insisting on the unprecedented and singular nature of the Shoah as an event and yet still using the most lurid formal tropes and common-place literary conventions to narrate it.

It is because of its concern with just these kinds of contradictions that sideshadowing is so useful a concept. In their retrospective ina-bility to imagine that any options existed for the Jews before the 1930s and, more damaging still, in their unwillingness to imagine the al-ternatives which the Jews of that era imagined for themselves except by pathologizing their hopes as willful delusions or symptoms of self-hatred, determinist histories impose a reductively monolithic frame-work upon an astonishingly rich and heterogenous subject matter. Such determinism inevitably pronounces its certainties in a tone that E. P. Thompson powerfully labeled "the enormous condescension of posterity,"[32] and part of what I wish to do in this study is to help rescue from such condescension the culture and personal decisions of the communities that were obliterated.

What is required to begin resolving the antinomy Katz describes, which I have extended into the discourse of the Shoah as a whole, is to register honestly, without the acquired certainty of backshadowing or the tone of patronizing incredulity to which it gives rise, that there is nothing self-evidently deluded in the fact that it was the *wrong* pre-diction, the fatally *incorrect* interpretation of public events that won the intellectual and emotional allegiance of the vast majority of Euro-pean Jews. Or to phrase the issue still more starkly: the wrong pre-diction did not have to be wrong, and its failure was, if anything, a good deal less likely than the (retrospectively) more accurate Zionist prognosis. Thus, even someone with as complex and ambivalent a relationship to European Jewish history as Hannah Arendt is both more persuasive and more fair than many of her critics when she writes about pre-World War I Vienna that the anti-Semitism of Mayor Karl Lueger's Christian-Social Party "remained without consequence; the decades when Lueger ruled Vienna were actually a kind of golden age for the Jews."[33] Of course Arendt, composing these sentences in the immediate aftermath of the war, does so with a full awareness of how hollow that "golden age" really was and how quickly Lueger's more brutal descendants would transform his rhetoric of Jew-baiting into daily practice. But what Arendt does not permit herself here, although she comes perilously close in her polemically backshadowing *Eichmann in Jerusalem*, is to sneer at those who believed in their security under Habsburg law and who refused to be frightened into flight by the election of Europe's first populist anti-Semitic mayor. Surprisingly enough, Arendt's and Zweig's judgments about a "golden age" for Austria's Jews are also echoed by S. Y. Agnon (1888–1970), who is widely regarded as the greatest Hebrew novelist of the century. A lifelong Zionist, Agnon was deeply sensitive to the dangers of assimilationism, but in a novella like "Betrothed," set in pre-World War I Palestine, for example, the narrator describes his protagonist's state of mind in these terms: "Jacob Rechnitz was a native of Austria, where one is less conscious of the Exile and where one's thoughts are drawn to happier things."[34] Since the story was first published in 1943, well after the German annexation of Austria (*Anschluss*),[35] Agnon certainly knew the fragility of such happiness, but for all the irony of his description, he refuses to judge his characters in terms of later events they could never have anticipated. The difference between, on the one hand, a perspective dominated by backshadowing and, on the other, one that respects the variety in how people understood their own positions and the contradictory expectations with which communities debated important decisions, turns on what Frederic Maitland defined as the first rule for comprehending history: an awareness that events now far in the past were once in the future.

One reason why Maitland's formulation is so important to a theory of sideshadowing is that it helps bring into focus the decisive differences between my position in this study and that of works like Danto's *Analytical Philosophy of History.* Although I have gratefully seized upon Danto's jest about Mme. Diderot, it is important to acknowledge that unlike Ignatieff, Danto is not arguing that historians should "write history blind to the future," even if such a thing were possible. On the contrary, he stresses that while an account of Diderot's subsequent career would make no sense if uttered by Mme. Diderot or by a hypothetical angel attending Denis's birth, some such judgment is unavoidable for later historians. Only after, and precisely *because,* subsequent events have occurred (in this case, Diderot's career as a writer and encyclopaedist) can we give a description of his early life that is grounded, if only implicitly, in a recognition that the subject of the study grew into a major thinker and author. Danto further implies that without a knowledge of later events, any historical account may be seriously inadequate and incomplete. But he is equally at pains to warn against histories that include "descriptions of events . . . which make an essential reference to later events—events future to the time at which the description is given. In effect [such works] are trying to write the history of what happens *before* it has happened, and to give accounts of the past based upon accounts of the future."[36] Phrased in this way, it becomes clear that the issue is determined precisely by the intended chronological scope and ideological/moral assumption of a specific historical account. In terms of my argument here, I believe that only when narratives about pre-Shoah European Jewry are able to incorporate the different ways individuals evaluated their circumstances at the time, and do so without flaunting a foreknowledge of the impending catastrophe, can a genuine sense of grief, unadulterated by anger or condescension at the "inevitable" truth that went unnoticed, be heard clearly.

A history of European Jewry that continues into the Nazi period obviously must include a detailed discussion of the Shoah, but (1) if the story stops earlier, for example at the end of World War I, it need not allow, and indeed, may only be deflected by allowing the knowledge of the coming genocide to structure its account of the prior epoch; and (2) even when the narrative makes the Shoah central to its description, it should not use the author's and reader's knowledge of that catastrophe to impose the terms within which earlier events are analyzed. To return to Danto's example, our awareness of Diderot's career is undoubtedly the reason we are interested in his early years (unlike histories of a whole community, with individual biographies only the acknowledged importance, or at least representative character, of the whole life makes someone's first years a likely subject for a written reconstruction), but that awareness cannot be projected backward to anyone in Langres in 1715, nor can it be used legitimately to judge anyone's actions vis-à-vis Diderot during his years at home. Directly indebted to Danto, but still more committed to a theoretical horizon that appears to legitimize backshadowing, Jürgen Habermas insists that

> Historical accounts make use of narrative statements. They are called narrative because they present events as elements of stories [*Geschichten*]. Stories have a beginning and an end; they are held together by an action. Historical events are reconstructed within the reference system of a story. They cannot be presented without relation to other, later events. . . . Narrative statements describe an event with the aid of categories under which it could not have been observed. The sentence, "the Thirty Years War began in 1618," presupposes that at least those events have elapsed which are relevant for the history of the war up to the Peace of Westphalia, events that could not have been narrated by any observer at the outbreak of the war. . . . The predicates with which an event is narratively presented require the appearance of later events in the light of which the event in question appears as an historical event.[37]

One way to highlight the issue at stake here is to confront Habermas's account with a contrary formulation in which we imagine a German burgher running through town shouting, "The Thirty Years War has just begun!" The distinction, in other words, is not necessarily one of foreshadowing and backshadowing, but rather the horizon of consciousness and knowledge that one is seeking to describe. There is nothing wrong with a historian narrating events from the perspective of a time future to the subject matter and knowing more about that subject than its contemporaries could have—for example, the length of a given war—but such knowledge should not delude the historian into thinking that the future was inevitable simply because it happened, nor should it be used to judge the way contemporaries, existing without such information, viewed their own circumstances and decided upon particular courses of action. Moreover, and crucial to the theme of this book, both Habermas and Danto assume a curiously restrictive notion of what constitutes a "story." As we have already seen, both archaic and postmodern narratives show that stories need not have a single beginning and a single end; indeed, they need not even have a single, chronologically ordered series of actions. History can be understood as readily by these two earlier and later categories of narrative organization as by the linear, determined trajectory of a story that Habermas and Danto posit as the sole available model. We could rephrase Habermas by saying "stories need have no beginning or end; they are held together by actions and their sideshadows." But Habermas pushes his case still further by insisting both that historians *necessarily* use their greater knowledge to transcend the horizon of people actually involved in the story that is being told, and that the future be seen as somehow *intended* by the actions undertaken in the present:

> The historian does not observe from the perspective of the actor but describes events and actions out of the experiential horizon of a history that goes beyond the actor's horizons of expectations. But the meaning that retrospectively accrues to events in this way emerges only in the schema of possible action, that is, only if the events are viewed as if this meaning had—with the knowledge of those who were born later—been intended. . . . A series of events acquires the unity of a story only from a point of view that cannot be taken from those events themselves. The actors are caught in their histories; even for them—if they tell their own stories—the point of view from which the events can take on the coherence of a story arises only subsequently.[38]

But we should notice here again the assumption that a story has "coherence," by which Habermas means specifically the coherence of a classically shaped and closed narrative. The crux of the matter is that a certain view of history is being determined not so much by principles of historiography but by a prior and naive grasp of what constitutes a story *tout court.* If we reconceive our understanding of the possibilities of storytelling and entertain more flexibility in our possible models, if we do not insist on closure and the retrospective judgment that closure is allowed to dictate, then the point of view of any single moment in the trajectory of an ongoing story has a significance that is never annulled or transcended by the shape and meaning of the narrative as a (supposed) whole.[39]

The problem is that the particular flourishing of historical consciousness that began in the nineteenth century ended up by making the historian, or at least the thinker as historical system builder, whether in the form of a pure philosopher like Hegel, a philosophically trained revolutionary thinker and polemicist like Marx, or a conservative vulgarizer like Spengler, seem the one best equipped to interpret the world. But these kinds of historical analyses, especially when they are part of a larger philosophical vision, tend to legislate the future, as well as to explain the present and past, in terms of a single, coherent system whose laws the philosopher-historian has uncovered. The inevitability of these laws not only renders individual human creativity and freedom irrelevant, it also removes any significance from imagining alternative paths. Within such a logic, alternatives are "mere daydreams." The task for sideshadowing is to restore the legitimacy of reflecting upon what might have taken place instead.

What sideshadowing explicitly rejects is a certain view of how events assume meaning for us, a view perhaps most powerfully put by Wilhelm Dilthey:

> We grasp the significance of a moment of the past. It is significant insofar as a linkage to the future was achieved in it. . . . The individual moment [has] significance through its connection with the whole, through the relation of past and future. . . . But what constitutes the peculiar nature of this relation of part to whole within life? It is a relation that is never entirely completed. One would have to await the end of one's life and could only in the hour of death survey the whole from which the relation

of the parts could be determined. One would have to await the end of history to possess all the material needed for determining its significance.[40]

It is worth asking why it should be exclusively the end of the story that determines how one interprets everything that went before? How much of a specifically Christian theological perspective has been unwittingly imported into a historiographic context by this privileging of what sounds remarkably like a secular Last Judgment? To place such heavy weight upon "the end of one's life and . . . the hour of death" reveals this metamorphosis of a Christian topos with particular vividness. But one might just as well argue that everybody dies and that all nations and civilizations have at some point ended, so culmination, in the sense of termination, is both a commonplace and an uninformative universal truism. Why, then, should it be *the* sense-giving criterion for every stage that transpired before the inevitable end? The Roman Empire ultimately collapsed, but does its downfall make what happened during its lengthy existence meaningless or count only as a step toward the sacking of Rome by barbarians? Both on the personal biographical level and on the historical one, there is no reason to accept the retrospective authority of the last days. Dilthey's attitude here exactly parallels the point of view that the Shoah, as the death of the Austro-German Jewish community, must be understood as a judgment on that community, as the event by which everything earlier acquires its final sense. It is not the smallest irony of such arguments that, while arising from a perspective supposedly consonant with Jewish traditions and values, they actually rely on the deepest strands of a Christian metaphysics.[41]

But intimately linked, as it clearly is, to a sense of the importance of sideshadowing, the rejection of the sense-making authority of the future to determine how we interpret past events still leaves unspecified a way to clarify the difference between *prediction* and foreshadowing. A constituent part of our sense of the present moment is an imaginative investment in some of the futures that might come out of it. Because presentness already includes anticipation, prediction does not in itself violate the integrity of presentness. Some form of prediction is an inherent aspect of how we organize our world, affecting both greater and smaller plans, whether moment by moment or at decisive turning points. In prediction one makes the best guess possible about an *unknown* future, a guess limited by all the partiality of one's knowledge, temperament, and desire. But in both foreshadowing and backshadowing the writer continuously passes judgment on the characters' projects and predictions by drawing on the plenitude of his greater information about the end of the story. Since the writer knows which events "really mattered," which plans will bring disaster and which success, the existence of the book's subjects as human beings engaged in an ongoing effort to shape their own futures is denied any substantive meaning. In novels based on historical events known to both the author and reader, the narrative may *seem* concerned with registering the predictions of the characters. But the intrusion of foreshadowing, the network of portentous signs that signal the future of the characters and their world, is particularly deceptive because it is based upon the shared familiarity of a known outcome. In historical novels, unless the horizon is kept strictly within the consciousness of the characters themselves, any surplus of knowledge or interpretation is an instance of pure backshadowing from an already established future, even if, technically, it presents itself in the rhetorical modes of either prediction or foreshadowing.

To write about their forms of communal life, knowing that the Jews of Vienna's "golden age" were doomed, and then to blame them for not having realized it themselves in time to escape, is to attribute a far greater clarity and monologic shrillness to contemporary warning signs than they actually warranted. Danger signals obviously existed in significant quantities, but so did countless contradictory and, in the main, reassuring ones, and there is nothing inherently surprising that it should have been the latter that most people chose to believe. To illustrate this problem, one need only consider the sordid career of Georg Ritter von Schönerer (1842–1921), standard-bearer for the most extreme Austrian anti-Semitic party of his day and one of Hitler's acknowledged heroes. In 1888, Schönerer and a gang of thugs smashed up the office of the Jewish-owned, liberal newspaper *Neues Wiener Tageblatt* and beat up some of the staff, including the editor, Moritz Szeps.[42] About this incident, Ignatieff poses the telling question: "Is the historian to emphasize the anticipatory echo of the 1930s? Or should emphasis be placed on the fact that Schönerer was arrested, convicted, stripped of his title and his seat as a deputy, and sent to prison for four months?"[43] Ignatieff's argument is so appealing for a theory of sideshadowing that there is a strong temptation to adopt it in its entirety. But there is a risk that by formulating the question in terms of a rigid either/ or choice, Ignatieff may be overcorrecting against the dangers of backshadowing and introducing a different kind of simplification of his own. To deny any link between Schönerer and Hitler is as dubious a move as to see them in a deterministic continuum. A politically successful Nazi movement required numerous predecessors to prepare the ground for its ideology, as well as specific and distinct local conditions to make that success a reality. Hitler could not have been taken seriously as a political leader without a history of anti-Semitic *völkisch* demagogues like Schönerer to prepare the ground, but the path from one to the other was not foreseeable, let alone inevitable.[44] Thus when Herzl in 1895 describes the Viennese joy at Lueger's mayoral victory with the memorable image of a man in the crowd standing next to him fervently declaring, "That is our Führer,"[45] chilling though subsequent history has made the phrase, it is essential not to be so hypnotized by the negative aura of the Nazi Reich as to miss precisely what Herzl himself heard in the words: the voice of a triumphant and irredeemable Austrian anti-Semitism, not a *figura* of the later mob wildly cheering the arrival of Germany's Führer returning home to the Vienna he had just conquered.[46] In Berel Lang's elegant formulation, "Affiliation does not amount to inevitability; what is latent does not have to become manifest."[47]

Unlike Ignatieff's recommendation of deliberate blindness to the future, sideshadowing does not treat each moment of history as a monad, unconnected to what preceded or followed: a strictly atomistic view of history presupposes a relationship to time as distorted as the deterministic one that is its mirror image. Nor does sideshadowing argue against relationships and consequences evolving over time; it says only that few of these consequences are either necessary or

consistently predictable, and it urges that the multiple choices of action available at a given moment, and the realization that the present
contains the seeds of diverse and mutually exclusive possible futures,
be included in one's understanding of what any single moment entails. In the case of Schönerer, sideshadowing would argue that a
crucial element in any history of his movement is how the Jewish
community of Vienna and the rest of the Empire viewed both the
threat he presented and the significance of his legal disgrace. The
episode seems to have encouraged and solidified what was already a
powerful tendency among many of the more prosperous Jews toward
a certain nervous conservatism and faith in the Emperor as a bulwark
against populist and rabble-rousing anti-Semitism. Schönerer's failure, far from making the Empire's Jews blindly complacent about
their safety, as the most vulgar versions of backshadowing history fan-
tasize, encouraged them to look for their security in those institutions
that seemed, reasonably enough, to offer the greatest potential for
protecting their welfare. It was only when all those institutions themselves crumbled that this decision proved disastrous, but the social
and legal disintegrations that preceded the assumption of state power
by virulently anti-Semitic forces was not a prediction that either the
Schönerer affair or Lueger's successful career as mayor could be expected to have let anyone foresee.[48]

In George Clare's memoirs of his secularized Austro-Jewish family
there is a revealing indication of how past experiences were invoked
by Viennese Jews to reassure themselves not only after Hitler's assumption of power in Germany but even after the Nazi *Anschluss* of
Austria. Both the author's father and grandfather had suffered injustice under Lueger by being refused timely promotions and university posts. But in their circle not one Jew had been physically
harmed, and even the career injuries had been slight and were ultimately rectified. Most of Vienna's Jews in the early 1930s thought
Hitler would be like Lueger, rabble-rousing during election cam-
paigns but relatively temperate once in office.[49] Clare sees his grand-
mother's reaction to the *Anschluss* as typical of her generation:
"Growing up and maturing in the heyday of European Liberalism
[they] could envisage some aspects of evil, something of Lueger's

treatment of [Jews] . . . but [they] could neither envisage nor comprehend the brutal evil that was breaking out all over Vienna that very day."[50] In Lawrence Langer's extraordinary analysis of taped interviews made with survivors of the Shoah, he quotes a historian who has tried to come to terms with this same question and concluded that "we build our expectations of the future . . . on our familiarity with the past. How could we foresee gas chambers . . . when we had never heard of them?"[51]

Nor is this situation unique to Austro-German Jewry. A similar debate has arisen in France about the degree of self-consciousness of the French Jews as a separate—and endangered—community in the decade before the anti-Semitic legislation and deportations of the Vichy years. Emmanuel Berl (1892–1976), an assimilated Jewish intellectual and writer, related to the Proust and Bergson families with whom he associated as a young man, confronted this issue shortly before his death in an interview conducted by Patrick Modiano. To Modiano, born after the Shoah and centrally engaged with its implications for his own identity, Berl's refusal to see how grave the danger was in the 1930s seems almost incomprehensible. But Berl's answer is a gentle rebuke about how different history looks if one is predicting rather than backshadowing. In his own defense, Berl quietly points out that his generation of bourgeois Jews saw no reason to fear for their lives during the rising anti-Semitism of the late 1920s and 1930s. After all, Berl argues, they had already endured the most virulent episode of officially encouraged anti-Semitism they could imagine—the Dreyfus affair—and survived it with only verbal abuse and social discrimination, but no actual physical harm. Thus, when new waves of what initially seemed like the same madness broke out, they naturally turned to history and communal memory for guidance and found sufficient reason to think that this latest episode would also pass without jeopardizing their survival. Here too, the distinction is that for contemporary writers the legacy of anti-Semitism culminates "inevitably" in Auschwitz; for Berl's contemporaries it led, just as inevitably, to the public crises and confrontations of the Dreyfus period.[52] Of all the contradictions we have been tracing, there is one so deeply and unreflectively embedded in most accounts of the Shoah that it has become an almost indispensable cornerstone of narratives about the genocide. On the one hand, this contradictory perspective insists that the Shoah was an absolutely unprecedented event in human history, while on the other hand, it blames Europe's assimilated Jews for not having anticipated, and thus avoided, the plan for their total extermination. Without the acerbity of polemics, both Clare and Berl try to make us see how carelessly dismissive of the realities confronted by their generation such a judgment is, and how destructive of any genuine historical understanding are backshadowing's certainties.

Earlier in this section, I spoke with what might have seemed excessive disgust at the increasingly common literary topos of Hitler's birth as a sort of daemonic nativity. But by now it ought to be apparent that there is a sense in which historical backshadowing unwittingly places the pre-war European Jews in a position disturbingly similar to the one assigned them by the early Church. Just as the first Christians condemned the Jews for having seen the Savior, witnessed his miracles, and still choosing to reject him, so the contempt of writers projecting backward from their knowledge of the Shoah convicts all those who failed to heed the initial signs of Nazism's reign. It is as though the Jews, initially cursed for not recognizing the Messiah, are now to be scorned again, two millennia later, for having failed to recognize the anti-Christ. To have been blind to "the truth" at Bethlehem and at Braunau, to have misrecognized first the eternal promise incarnated in the carpenter's son and then the mortal peril in the custom inspector's, are the terms to which Jewish history is reduced once its content is held accountable to the certainties visible from the standpoint of backshadowing.

But the problem raised here is hardly amenable to global rules or absolute standards. What constitutes a reasonable warning sign is very much an open question, and no matter what answer one gives, it is hardly likely to be the same in 1913 as in 1933.

That many Jewish writers, and not only dedicated Zionists, realized the precariousness of their position is clear from a novel like Arthur Schnitzler's fascinating *The Road to the Open,* originally published in 1908 in six installments in the journal *Neue Rundschau.* The novel incorporates a number of powerful debates between Viennese Zionist and anti-Zionist Jews, and shows how all of them were keenly aware of the growing anti-Semitism in Austria, but differed both in their estimation of the danger it represented and in their plans for the best means to combat/escape it.[53] In one of the most impressive of these scenes, the issue of a supposed Jewish "oversensitivity" and "persecution mania" arises, prompting an outburst that is all the more powerful for its insight, not just into a *future* threat faced by Austrian Jewry, but into the daily risks to their well-being and self-esteem that Jews incurred living in a city that had always, in varying degrees, despised them:

> Do you think there's a single Christian in the world, even taking the noblest, straightest, and truest one you like, one single Christian who has not in some moment or other of spite, temper or rage, made at any rate mentally some contemptuous allusion to the Jewishness of even his best friend, his mistress or his wife, if they were Jews or of Jewish descent? . . . And as for talking about persecution-mania, why it would be much more logical to talk about a mania for being hidden, a mania for being left alone, a mania for being safe; which though perhaps a less sensational form of disease is certainly a much more dangerous one for its victims.[54]

Although I have emphasized that we must read Schnitzler's warning in terms of the Habsburg Vienna his characters inhabit, it would be dishonest to pretend it is easy to come across these lines without the shadow of the Nazi era darkening them beyond anything the author dreamed of. But we need to make just such an effort in order not to judge Schnitzler's characters by future facts of which they could have had no inkling. The plight of the Jews in *The Road to the Open* is serious enough to engage us on its own terms without requiring any additional peril to rivet our attention. Schnitzler never imagined the Shoah when he wrote *The Road to the Open,* and his character is offering both a diagnosis of a present danger and a (significantly imprecise) prognosis of the serious risk for anyone exposed to that peril, but there is no backshadowing in the novel since neither the writer nor his intended reader possesses a knowledge denied to the figures in the book itself. *We,* the post-war readers of the novel, import—

illicitly, but I suspect unavoidably—our knowledge into the world of
Schnitzler's Vienna. As long as we recognize that it is solely *our* awareness, not the text's, that makes us respond to the characters' debates
as though they were taking place against a backdrop of what will
become a pathologically genocidal anti-Semitism, our temptation to
backshadow can be held in check by the novel's own openness toward
the still-to-be-determined future.

To *write* history blind to the future is less difficult than to *read* it
blind to the past that has intervened since the time of the narrative.
But I think the importance of doing so increases in proportion to the
difficulty it entails, a difficulty that is really one of forming a single
perspective within which both the historical and the moral imagination are fused and which allows us to acknowledge the authenticity
of values and decisions alien to our own. Only from within this perspective, one not determined by a knowledge of the future, can we
listen to the conflicting voices of the past with equal attentiveness.
Schnitzler is no more a prophet of the Shoah than was Kafka, and
his very lack of prophetic certainty enabled him to register with precision and empathy the different and contradictory projections into
the future of the multifarious Viennese Jewish bourgeois intelligentsia. What backshadowing can never attempt without condescension
is the most richly instructive aspect of Schnitzler's book for readers
today. It lets us hear the reasonableness of those who made the fatally
wrong guesses, recording their position with the same degree of sympathetic clarity as it does the arguments of characters who turned out
to be more accurate in their predictions:

> "My own instinct . . . tells me infallibly that my home is here, just here,
> and not in some land which I don't know, the description of which
> doesn't appeal to me the least bit and which certain people now want to
> persuade me is my fatherland on the strength of the argument that that
> was the place from which my ancestors some thousand years ago were
> scattered into the world." . . . National feeling and religion, those had
> always been the words which had embittered him. . . . And so far as relig-
> ions were concerned, he liked Christian and Jewish mythology quite as
> much as Greek and Indian; but as soon as they began to force their dog-
> mas upon him he found them all equally intolerable and repulsive. . . .

And least of all would the consciousness of a persecution which they had all suffered, and of a hatred whose burden fell upon them all, make him feel linked to men from whom he felt himself so far distant in temperament. He did not mind recognizing Zionism as a moral principle and a social movement, . . . but the idea of the foundation of a Jewish state on a religious and national basis struck him as a nonsensical defiance of the whole spirit of historical evolution.[55]

Schnitzler's Jewish characters fiercely and obsessively debate both what it means to be an Austrian Jew and what solution would be best for their embattled position. At various times, all of the novel's Jewish characters are targets of open anti-Semitism, but unlike contemporary clichés about a pandemic "Jewish self-hatred" among secularized Austro-German Jews, only a very few of them show any inclination to disguise, let alone to renounce, their Jewishness.[56] Irrespective of any shared experiences of racial discrimination, their circumstances and temperaments are sufficiently various to militate against their agreeing on a single course of action. Instead, each character reacts quite differently in accordance with the dense network of personal ambitions, hopes, schemes, and ideals that are part of his nature.

This is exactly what sideshadowing is intended to illuminate, and it is integral to any notion of human freedom. It was Nazism that denied Jews any right to choose their identity or degree of communal affiliation, reducing all Jews to a single, undifferentiated category with one common destiny. For the Nazis and, with only a modification of the criteria of judgment, the Communists (for the race into which one was born, Communism merely substitutes the class), history was monologic as well as monolithic: the impulse toward individual choices, with its attendant debates and uncertainties, was regarded by both as the Jewish ("talmudic") vice *par excellence*. Sideshadowing is certainly not an especially Jewish principle, either historically or methodologically, but one can say that it is a fundamentally democratic and pluralistic one, and that, whether they label themselves "progressive" or "*völkisch*," it is totalitarian ideologies that are in principle most deeply resistant to admitting the validity of sideshadowing.

John Dewey, voicing the pragmatist's view of historiography, argued that an "intelligent understanding of past history is to some extent a lever for moving the present into a certain kind of future. . . . In using what has come to them as an inheritance from the past [people] are compelled to modify it to meet their own needs, and this process creates a new present in which the process continues. History cannot escape its own process. It will, therefore, always be rewritten."[57] In spite of the sharp critiques provoked by such a viewpoint, finding a "usable past" (i.e., locating in the community's history a fund of useful *exempla* with which to instigate present changes) is a powerful urge in many narrative histories, especially those composed during a time when the writer feels the physical, economic, or cultural welfare of his own people to be imperiled.[58] Such a view need not imply that the information thus selected is not also objectively true (that is, as accurate as any purely contingent and humanistic study can hope to be), only that all historical knowledge is selected and then presented according to the criteria, consciously acknowledged or not, of the historian's own interests and passions. Only from the impossible vantage point of an ultimate clarity (whether it take the form of a Messianic Last Judgment or the attainment of a secular historical perfectionism) can history be comprehended as a totality, a grand summary in which everything is recognized in its true value and all the earlier events are harmonized within the plenitude of a final synthesis. In human terms there simply is no privileged horizon from which history can be seen clearly and recorded whole. History does not unfold through a homogeneous time that can be surveyed *sub specie aeternitatis.* Whether its form be a detailed monograph, an extended chronological survey, or a fictional narrative, what emerges from an intense concern for history is always something like a dynamic image or vortex, a series of intertwined crystallizations or illuminations, vitally bound to the particular concerns of the perceiver. But as Walter Benjamin reminds us, far from being an index of unreliability, the very "partiality" (in both senses) of each perception is a necessary aspect of its continuing human significance: "For every image of the past that is not recognized by the present as one of its own concerns threatens to disappear irretrievably." [59]

But if, in their different ways, both Dewey's and Benjamin's arguments, based more on ethical than epistemological claims, have any validity, they raise a troubling question for sideshadowing that is quite different from the one posed by Danto and Habermas: is it right to demand that a writer ignore indications of future problems when composing an account of a historical life or movement, if those problems only manifested themselves with any force much later than the period treated in the narrative? It seems to me that some form of retrospective analysis is not only humanly irresistible, but theoretically legitimate as well. For example, there is no doubt that Palestinian grievances, especially since the *intifada,* have made historians go back and examine more closely the contemporary documents showing how the early Zionists envisaged the Jews and Arabs getting along in the new Jewish state. Thus, Ernst Pawel's ineradicable attraction to seeing the past in terms of the future that issued from it has a different, and more defensible, function in his biography of Theodor Herzl, *The Labyrinth of Exile,* than in the Kafka one. It is true that a reliance on vulgar psychological theorizing characterizes both books. For example, Pawel links Herzl's brief fascination with gambling during his university years to his later willingness to take daring risks for the Zionist cause, and attributes Herzl's attraction to second-rate authors to his mother's defective aesthetic judgments, describing her as "probably responsible for some genetic damage to her son's taste in literature and the arts."[60] But the kind of psychological foreshadowing that is so dubious in the biography of an individual has an entirely distinct—and methodologically less questionable—status when the issue becomes one of assessing a political program or theory. Pawel emphasizes how Herzl regularly ignored Arab realities, thinking that there were few Arabs in Palestine to begin with and that those already there would gladly sell their land to the Jews. Herzl repeatedly refused to pay attention to reports by his own emissary to Palestine, the Ukrainian mathematician and Zionist leader Leo Motzkin (1867–1933), because Motzkin reluctantly concluded that the Arabs occupied the most fertile areas and were determined not to give them up, irrespective of the price offered.[61] Pawel, judging from the perspective of post-1967 Israel, makes Herzl's blindness to the potential gravity of the problem a central strand in his biography. And yet, although troubling, such a method does not warrant the kind of theoretical criticism that was appropriate when he applied it to Kafka's life. When Pawel points out that Kafka's sisters would be killed in a concentration camp near where they once visited their sick brother, this link is entirely fortuitous and unrelated to any of the sisters' decisions or acts. But if Herzl deliberately disregarded reports on the Arab population's likely resistance to Jewish immigration, his error, even if its consequence only became apparent years later, was a direct outgrowth of his initial assumptions and of the policy based upon them.[62] Pawel's highlighting of today's Arab-Jewish problem in his analysis of early Zionist debates is not a true case of backshadowing because the indications of future problems, if not their full implications, were clearly available to Herzl, and hence the perspective adopted by Pawel to judge Herzl's decisions is consonant with criticisms already apparent and articulated in Herzl's own time.

A preliminary account of why the effects of backshadowing differ according to the kind of history that is being told would stress that political programs always project themselves into the future and thus ask from their very inception to be judged by the criterion of future results. But whenever backshadowing vitiates the immediate context in which political projects were conceived, then those histories whose judgments are determined by the knowledge as well as the needs of the historian's present cannot be justified even by an appeal to Dewey's overly flexible model.

Although Ignatieff's criterion of willed blindness to future consequences may be impossibly demanding, it is an essential premise of sideshadowing that the immediate reality of an individual must be grasped on its own terms without the radical simplification of alternatives that characterizes a purely retrospective judgment. Backshadowing's selective interpretation of the past is designed to establish only the inevitability of subsequent developments, thus removing precisely the element of struggle for an ever-evolving significance in both past and present. In the case of Austro-German Jewry, backshadowing does not find new significance in the past but rather denies that it had any significance to begin with; instead of finding a "usable past," it is concerned almost exclusively with writing the moralizing tale of a "useless past" whose destruction in the Shoah was only the most brutal proof of its essential unfitness to survive.

The cruelty of backshadowing can be illustrated concisely by realizing that it regards as pointless the lives of countless numbers of people over hundreds of years like the Polish or Austro-German Jews who contributed to the building and maintenance of the synagogues that were eventually razed by the Nazis. Each present, and each separate life, has its own distinct value that later events cannot wholly take away, and we must, it seems to me, believe this in order to continue to have any conviction about our own actions and plans.

Ultimately, what is at issue here for communal memory has to do with nuances of proportion, stance, and tone. These, in turn, are part of how each writer works out the relationship between the individual fates of his characters and the collective trauma of European Jewry. All of these questions together constitute what we might call the difficult search for "decorum," but the last aspect is especially problematic because both the individual and the community as a whole are so deeply involved in trying to make sense of and interpret what is always called, by a kind of instinctive first reaction, the senselessness of the Shoah. And it is this dialectic, the tension between the senselessness of genocide and the sense-making urge of narrative, that centrally engages the theme of historical inevitability versus sideshadowing with which my discussion began.

3

NARRATING THE SHOAH

And he is a witness whether he has seen or known
of it; if he does not utter it, then he shall bear his
iniquity.

Leviticus 5:1

Ignorance about those who have disappeared under-
mines the reality of the world.

Zbigniew Herbert,
"Mr. Cogito on the Need for Precision"

At a dinner party several years ago, two of my colleagues began a
debate to whose complex and charged arguments I listened with riv-
eted attention and to which I have often returned in my own thinking. Both these close friends were from the last two generations of
brilliant, secularized German-Jewish intellectuals whose cultural so-
phistication and wide-ranging learning make clear the provincialism
of most contemporary intellectual discourse. What they argued about
was the ethical status of "Holocaust fiction," whether in books, plays,
or on film. One of them, the late Leo Lowenthal, echoing his lifelong
friend and co-worker Theodor Adorno, insisted that *all* fictionalizations, no matter how scrupulously accurate their research, were inherently pernicious because they could not help introducing an element of "aesthetic gratification" alongside of, but also structurally
integral with, their presentation of the horrific subject of the Shoah.
Only the most strictly factual historical studies, the memoirs of survivors, the diaries, notebooks, and sketches of the victims, or interviews with those directly involved seemed to him not to risk making
an "entertainment" out of the agony of Hitler's victims. I quote

Adorno's well-known version of this position because his formulation encapsulates a widely shared response to questions concerning how, and indeed whether, to represent the Shoah. Adorno warns of the "barbarism" inherent in "the so-called artistic representation" of the pain of those who have been tortured because any such representation "contains the power ... to extract pleasure out of it. ... Through aesthetic principles of stylization ... the unimaginable ordeal appears as if it had some meaning; it is transfigured and stripped of some of its horror and this in itself already does an injustice to the victims."[1]

The other side of that debate was maintained by a classicist, Thomas Rosenmeyer, from whose scholarly learning and humane curiosity I have often directly benefited. But on that occasion, his strenuous defense of the right of authors to represent the Shoah in their fictions, and his insistence that for all its singularity, the Nazi genocide was as proper a subject for narrative retelling as any other historical event, struck me as unconvincing. The incommensurability between the experiences to be represented and the means of representation, the unattainability of any fitting decorum to mediate between the author's words and the world of the Shoah, appeared to me absolute, even though I was never persuaded by Adorno's argument that artistic representation is an "injustice done to the victims." But the risk that fictional representations of the Shoah will be absorbed by what Leo Bersani, writing more globally but also, I think, less luridly than Adorno, has called "the culture of redemption," seemed to me a genuine one. Underwriting a redemptive view of art is the assumption that "a certain type of repetition of experience in art repairs inherently damaged or valueless experience. Experience may be overwhelming, practically impossible to absorb, but it is assumed ... that the work of art has the authority to master the presumed raw material of experience in a manner that uniquely gives value to, perhaps even redeems, that material."[2] The hazards described by both Adorno and Bersani appear to leave a certain thematically weighted and deliberately chosen silence as the only ethically unsullied response that art can make to the Shoah.

But in spite of the appeal of such a principled silence, I became

increasingly convinced that categorically refusing to represent the
Shoah in fiction is a far more menacing position. On one level, I
found myself resistant to the idea that anyone, whether a survivor of
the camps or not, should undertake to speak for the whole category
of Hitler's victims and generalize a set of principles, whether ethical,
religious, or aesthetic, on their behalf. Such a scruple troubled me
not only with regard to Adorno's formulation, but still more forcefully with Emil Fackenheim's attempt to derive a new, 614th commandment for contemporary Jewry that takes account of its situation after
the genocide. In the original wording of his 614th commandment,
Fackenheim, perhaps the most distinguished philosopher of the
Shoah, proclaims, "*The authentic Jew of today is forbidden to hand Hitler
yet another, posthumous victory.*"[3] To the scarcely disguised coerciveness
of Fackenheim's taking upon himself the decision of who are "authentic" Jews, and then enjoining upon them the requirement to live
their Jewishness to the full precisely in order to deny Hitler a "posthumous victory," a frivolous answer might be that having contested
most of the earlier 613 commandments, it is hardly surprising that
Jews would not be particularly eager to embrace a new one. But beyond the dubiousness of promulgating new commandments, there is
something that cries out to be resisted in Fackenheim's invocation
of the murdered babies and *Muselmänner*[4] of Auschwitz in his writing.
No one can speak for those murdered, and no one can determine
what would count as a further betrayal of their suffering. The freedom to choose—one's own philosophy, faith, communal affiliation,
and historical sense, as well as one's mode of remembering and representing that memory—is precisely what Nazism made impossible
for Jews, and although the affirmation of that freedom can do nothing for the victims of the Shoah, it is the only coherent rejection of
the Nazi principle of nondifferentiation among Jews.

But to focus specifically on the issue of the moral legitimacy of
aesthetic representation of the Shoah, I suspect that almost everyone
who has wrestled with this question and decided against any prohibition of fictionalizations has come up with similar arguments. Nonetheless, it is important to make explicit the basis of one's conclusions.

For me, the following considerations finally prevailed over my initial agreement with Adorno's interdiction.

Since the generation of survivors will soon die out, to prohibit anyone who was not actually caught in the Shoah from representing it risks consigning the events to a kind of oblivion interrupted only occasionally by the recitation of voices from an increasingly distant past. Any tribal story, if it is to survive as a living part of communal memory, needs regularly to be retold and reinterpreted. To keep silent would be still worse than a necessarily denaturing, because too "composed," speech, since it was precisely with the permanent silence of universal disbelief that the SS used to taunt the Jews in the camps—if any prisoners were to survive, the Nazis boasted, no one would believe their account. "Many survivors," Primo Levi writes, "remember that the SS militiamen enjoyed cynically admonishing the prisoners: 'However this war may end, we have won the war against you; none of you will be left to bear witness, but even if someone were to survive, the world will not believe him. There will perhaps be suspicions, discussions, research by historians, but there will be no certainties, because we will destroy the evidence together with you. And even if some proof should remain and some of you survive, people will say that the events you describe are too monstrous to be believed: they will say that they are the exaggerations of Allied propaganda and will believe us, who will deny everything, and not you. We will be the ones to dictate the history of the Lagers.' "[5] Even among themselves, the SS usually maintained a complex rhetoric of indirection, bureaucratese, paranomasia, euphemism, and displacement when referring to the Shoah. Thus, for example, the murder squads organized by Heydrich were called *Einsatzgruppen* (task forces) while the delicate phrase *Sonderbehandlung* (special treatment) was the standard term for physical annihilation. Even in Himmler's notorious speech of October 3, 1943, delivered to his senior officers at Posen, he first carefully refers to the *Judenevakuierung* (the "evacuation" or "deportation" of the Jews) before calling it *die Ausrottung* (extermination). Himmler announces that the genocide constitutes "ein niemals geschriebenes und niemals zu schreibenes Ruhmesblatt unserer Geschichte'' (a never-written and never-to-be-written page of glory in our [SS] history) and declares that although he will, this one time, discuss it openly (''Unter uns soll es einmal ganz offen ausgesprochen sein''), nonetheless it can never be talked about in the outside world (''und trotzdem werden wir in der Öffentlichkeit nie darüber reden'').[6] It is by public words, not by silence, that Himmler's boast is rejected, and in this sense, the retelling by other voices, voices of those who were never in German hands, crystallizes the continuing legacy of the Shoah, and confirms its wider importance as part of our collective memory.

Secondly, even the most scrupulous first-person ''factual'' testimony does a certain injustice to the other victims, if only by making its narrator the primary observing consciousness of both the tale and the events, thereby slighting the anguish of everyone else to a certain degree. Since survival itself was largely accidental, and since far more prisoners died in the camps than returned, the testimony of anyone who survived is necessarily both partial and, in the harshest sense, unrepresentative. (Primo Levi's *The Drowned and the Saved* [1986], for example, is haunted by the awareness that his own earlier account of Auschwitz, *If This Is a Man* [1947], is that of ''an anomalous minority,'' necessarily excluding the perspective of the vast majority of inmates who perished without leaving any record of their ordeal.)[7] Moreover, since one of the Nazi mechanisms of controlling the prisoners depended on isolating each of them as much and for as long as possible to keep them ignorant of the full scale of their predicament, the testimony of any single survivor, no matter how vivid and thoughtful, will be fragmentary and in need of supplementation from other sources and narratives. Indeed, Levi points out that most of the survivor narratives he has come across have already been influenced, often unconsciously, by ''information gathered from later readings or the stories of others.''[8] Even the seemingly strictest first-person narratives often bear *from the outset* the markings of other stories, other interpretations encountered after the Liberation, and bear those markings as part of the minimum necessity of being able to tell a story at all. As the Israeli author and concentration camp survivor Yehiel De-Nur (Ka-Tzetnik) makes clear, ''even those who had been there did not know Auschwitz. Not even someone who was there two long years, as I was."⁹ But in its turn, each "supplementary" narrative, whether fictional or "documentary," will itself also contain stylization, figurative language, aesthetic ordering, and a distinct point of view, and thus provide, amid the shock of the information it conveys, a certain formal "seemliness." If the text succeeds in moving its reader at all, then these writerly choices must have yielded a kind of readerly "pleasure," strange though the term may be in this context. Irrespective of the genre, a reader necessarily remains someone who responds with emotions and ideas to words encountered in a printed text, no matter how imaginatively unsettling the subject matter of the narrative.

Indeed, I think it is fair to argue that one of the most pervasive myths of our era, a myth perhaps even partially arising out of our collective response to the horrors of the concentration camps, is the absolute authority given to first-person testimony. Such narratives, whether by camp survivors or by those who have endured rape, child abuse, or any devastating trauma, are habitually regarded as though they were completely unmediated, as though language, gesture, and imagery could become transparent if the experience being expressed is sufficiently horrific. Testimony wrung out of a person under extreme duress is thus seen as the most true, the most unmediated, the most trustworthy. In contemporary aesthetics, for example, the force of much "performance art" relies precisely—and I think precariously—on just such a faith in the authenticity of first-person testimony. Indeed, it is not stretching a point to argue that recent American art in general has been marked by a strong, even if unconscious, Platonic suspicion of aesthetic mediation, imitation, and stylization. Often this mistrust takes the form of a new kind of Puritanism directed against style-as-artifice and against the imagination as being able to give shape to experiences not autobiographically grounded. But the severity of the suspicion at the claims of the imagination is balanced by an utterly naive faith in first-person narratives, as though they were "really true" and untouched by figuration and by the shaping of both conscious and unconscious designs on the speaker's part. Adorno's injunction against representing Shoah experiences in fic-

tion *because of the attendant stylization* assumes that testimonial accounts
have no such stylization, which is, of course, only a specific example
of what has become an increasingly prevalent criterion of judgment.
So deep-rooted has the anxiety of figuration become that even a recent memoir, *A Time to Speak*, by Helen Lewis, a Theresienstadt and
Auschwitz survivor, is accompanied by a foreword assuring the reader
that the book contains no novelistic "tricks." More surprisingly still,
the foreword, which bristles with scorn at literary self-consciousness,
is written by Jennifer Johnston, herself one of Ireland's more distinguished contemporary novelists: "All the baggage of the novelist is
here—joy and despair, good and evil, death and survival—but there
is no fiction, none of the novelist's attention-seeking tricks, nothing
is manipulated as a novelist would manipulate, the pattern is inherent
not imposed. Helen Lewis . . . never invents; there is only Truth, witnessed Truth."[10]

Yet surely there is no reason to assume that first-person testimony
about the horrific is more unmediated and complete than any other
kind of speech. For example, concentration camp victims have many
reasons, both conscious and unconscious, to amend and shape their
narratives (guilt about having survived at all, shame for any acts they
committed that may have been essential to their survival but which
deeply violated the ethics of their ordinary lives, and even a degree
of traumatization so severe as to make them incapable of recalling
crucial aspects of their own experience). If, for instance, as the Israeli
Supreme Court ruled on July 29, 1993, there is reasonable ground
to doubt that John Demjanjuk really was "Ivan the Terrible" of Tre-
blinka, then the misidentification by his surviving victims may be due
not only to the long interval between "Ivan's" acts and Demjanjuk's
arrest, but equally, to the very nature of the victims' suffering, which
made them perhaps *less* able to identify their tormentor correctly,
rather than, as the official myth has it, more certain of accurately
remembering him. Perhaps the very need to find, and see punished,
whoever made them suffer so terribly, persuaded the witnesses to
identify positively a likely, but not necessarily the correct, candidate.[11]
It is important to admit, moreover, that even the survivor-witness's
testimony moves us not just by its factual and evidentiary material,

but by fitting that material into a specific ideological/narrative framework. Readers respond very differently to autobiographical accounts of the Shoah, depending to a significant degree on the way the particular survivor's philosophical, religious, and socio-political perspectives color the documentary testimony. Primo Levi's liberal and scientifically trained Italian bourgeois worldview is unmistakably different from that of an Austrian literary intellectual like Hans Meyer (who wrote under the name Jean Améry after the war), let alone from that of an Eastern European Hasid, a Russian Bundist, or a committed Polish Zionist. All of the Shoah's victims may have shared the same fate, but as James Young rightly notes, "each victim 'saw'—i.e., understood *and* witnessed—his predicament differently, depending on his own historical past, religious paradigms, and ideological explanations." What we reconstruct through our reading is never the event as an absolute, but what Young goes on to call "the [contemporary writer's] understanding of them—that is, the epistemological climate in which they existed [for him] at the time."[12]

But so, too, every reader's response is shaped by the "epistemological climate" in which the testimony is read. As Jonathan Boyarin shrewdly observes, "in popular-culture representations of the Holocaust, the particular horror of the Nazi genocide is emphasized by an image of Jews as normal Europeans, 'just like us.' In fact we can only empathize with, *feel ourselves into,* those we can imagine as ourselves."[13] But the affective force of identification through perceived similarity is as powerful in high art as it is in popular culture. Secular Jewish intellectuals often react negatively, for example, to certain ultra-orthodox accounts of the Shoah (especially the theological explanation that it was the pre-war violation of the ritual laws and commandments by the assimilated Jews of Europe that was being expiated in the camps). Similarly, more religiously observant Jews often find Primo Levi's secular humanism shockingly blind to the anti-Semitic tendencies in the authors upon whom he drew for moral sustenance in Auschwitz. One of my colleagues, for example, told me that when he gave a talk on Levi's *Se questo è un uomo* to a local Jewish community, he was bitterly attacked by several members of the audience for praising the scene where the author rediscovers his fundamental humanity by recalling Dante's description of Ulysses in *Inferno* 26. Dante, in their eyes, was one of the central authors of the culture whose anti-Semitism had "culminated" in the camps, and they regarded Levi's invocation of Dante in such a setting as an index of an alienation from his people so complete that even Auschwitz could not teach him the futility of assimilationism. It is also instructive, if not particularly encouraging, to see that Levi is now under equally severe attack from quite a different source, not because of his lack of Jewish faith, but because he is so out of step with current American academic pieties. So, for example, Dominick LaCapra, a prominent history professor and theoretician, writes with breath-taking condescension, "It may also be useful to quote Levi on silence, for his words are instructive despite their dubious indebtedness to a largely unexamined tradition of high culture, overly analytic rationality, teleological assumptions and restrictive humanism."[14]

This disparity in responses should alert us to a fundamental paradox: all of the writers on the Shoah speak of its *incomprehensibility* and basic *incommunicability;* in fact, though, accounts of the Shoah, even more strictly than narratives of less extreme events, rely on the witness and his listener sharing the same code of values and explanatory models of individual and social behavior in order to render convincing the assertion that something "incommunicable" has been experienced. There is, in other words, no single order of memorable testimony, no transparent paradigm of representation, that can address the different narrative needs of all those gripped by the subject. Prohibitions of any kind inevitably—and futilely—try to erect the individual "legislator's" personal and ideological perspective as the only acceptable model.

Notwithstanding the extent to which theoretical reflection qualifies and ultimately rejects the insistence on purely factual narratives, the exploitation of the Nazi genocide in countless mediocre books and films is clearly a thoroughly depressing phenomenon. Revealingly though, the authors of many of the most clumsy fictionalizations are often at great pains in their prefaces or in separate interviews to insist that they have used the fullest available historical records and tried to be totally faithful to the facts as they have learned them through scrupulous research. In Thomas Keneally's *Schindler's List*, for example, we are told that the author has used "the texture and devices of the novel to tell a true story" and that he has wished "to avoid all fiction, since fiction would debase the record."[15] Berel Lang, who has discussed this issue with particular lucidity, notes that while the belief that "literature has moral presuppositions and consequences is not startling ... moral accountability has rarely been pressed against the writer for the very *act* of writing. . . . [Writers on the Shoah demonstrate a felt] obligation (morally, but also intellectually) to establish their *right* to address that event as a subject."[16] Critical to establishing this right, as Lang remarks in a subsequent study, is "not so much [the writers'] success in achieving historical authenticity, as their acknowledgment of that as a goal—their deference to the conventions of historical discourse as a literary means."[17] Implicit in all such arguments is the sense that while *no* actual testimony could "debase the record," *all* "fictionalizations" inevitably do so.

Yet there is an unexplored absence of correlation between the argument against literary stylization, which says that the element of aesthetic pleasure contradicts the meaningless horror of the Shoah, and the argument against fictionalization, which says that the figuration of events not directly experienced by the artist debases all those who actually have undergone them. Both of these positions are equally vulnerable, it seems to me, to one or more of the counterarguments outlined above, but the lack of any logical connection between the two principal injunctions against all representations not authenticated by direct experience is itself striking. Moreover, there is a phenomenon as depressing in its own way as the entertainment industry's commercialization of the Shoah, but which, because of the misplaced aura of wisdom with which we endow any survivors of such unprecedented suffering, has rarely been publicly discussed. I am thinking here of what George Steiner has described as the "disturbingly commercialized pathos of horror [that] has arisen around certain survivors and their all-too-eloquent and sometimes even theatrical witness."[18] But if the biographical veracity of testimony does not guarantee its ethical significance, and if the element of stylization is inherent in any representation, fictional or not, then there is actually no single, global issue or injunction to be debated. There is only a series of specific works including poems, films, sculptures, drawings, novels, historical studies, and autobiographical memoirs, each of whose seemliness needs to be considered on its own terms without recourse to any overarching formulae. Instead of a single problem, there are the constantly changing questions raised by each new work that addresses the Shoah, and instead of a set of criteria determined in advance, only a kind of extreme localism of attention can come to terms with the variety of ways the Shoah is figured in our historical and moral imaginations.

■   ■   ■

> We forgive the crimes of individuals, but not their participation in a collective crime.
>
> Marcel Proust, *Le Côté de Guermantes*

> "Patience, my dear, patience. If you listen to Bleiman you'll be warm, he's promising you paradise." "Is he promising a temperate climate too?" "No my dear, prophets don't talk about such petty details. They talk about the people, exile, and redemption." "All that has nothing to do with me," says Rita. "I need two warm blankets."
>
> Aharon Appelfeld, "1946"

Although everyone's list will surely differ, it is all too easy to think of representations of the Shoah whose lapses into tastelessness and exploitation are deeply offensive and which, in their vulgarity, risk coarsening the collective memory. But rare though they are, there is also a handful of works that have been painfully and movingly illuminating, whether semi-fictionalizations like Heinz Schirk's film of *The Wannsee Conference*, or, in Adorno's sense, "stylizations" as different from one another as Primo Levi's meditations on his concentration camp experiences and Dan Pagis's cycle of poems *Testimony*, or entirely imagined narratives like David Grossman's remarkable novel *See Under: Love*, as well as many of Alain Kleinmann's paintings and

Shimon Attie's photographs. The best of these, however, testify convincingly against an excessive insistence that *only* the gathering of facts has ethical validity—a kind of fetishization that is all the more insidious because, as the Czernovitz-born (1932), Israeli novelist Aharon Appelfeld cautions, "the numbers and the facts were the murderer's own well-proven means. Man as a number is one of the horrors of dehumanization."[19]

It is true that of the few authentically moving fictionalizations of the Shoah, even fewer are actually set inside the death camps, as though a kind of imaginative closure in the face of the horror made such scenes unrepresentable. The French writer Henri Raczymow, for example, links the twin themes of wondering about his right to speak about the Shoah as "neither victim, nor survivor, nor witness of the event"[20] with the logically subsidiary debate that asks: even if representation by someone not directly affected is judged permissible, how far can that representation go, what can it be allowed to figure and what must stay taboo? Raczymow's decision, made with trepidation and doubly mediated by the device of a fictitious chronicle kept by his narrator's sister, is that the world of the Warsaw Ghetto may be legitimate as a setting for the language of fiction, but the actual operation of a death camp must be excluded categorically from figural representation: "I see nothing. . . . I should not see anything. To want to see would place me beside the S.S. man in charge of looking through the peephole in order to see the condition of those being gassed."[21] It is hard not to sympathize with this distinction, but at the same time it also seems too arbitrary to be useful as a general rule. The method and setting of the genocide is not a very reliable demarcation point once the legitimacy of any literary representation has been allowed, and Raczymow's insistence on a strictly ethical criterion to determine where to place his narrator's eye may depend upon too elusive a distinction. If, for example, Raczymow himself had been a camp survivor like Tadeusz Borowski, whose collection of grimly sardonic stories, *This Way for the Gas, Ladies and Gentlemen,* shows the untenability of any fixed categories for literature about the Shoah, would the description of the gas chambers in operation be any less of a violation? But if not, why should the question of literary legitimacy depend on the biographical circumstances of the author?

Raczymow's hesitation is in part justified—and no doubt in part also motivated—by an awareness of how many recent works contain scenes set in the death factories in order to mobilize the emotions that such extreme situations elicit. The kind of *frisson* for which Pawel grasps by linking the births of Kafka's sister and Hitler bears a family resemblance to the way William Styron uses the Auschwitz scenes in *Sophie's Choice* to give his novel an intensity it would otherwise lack. And both of these in turn are not as far removed as their authors might think from the use of concentration camp settings as a staple of sadomasochistic pornography. But there is also another, and perhaps even more prevalent danger that haunts many readers of literature on the Shoah: that of becoming so caught up in the material that, compared with its intensities, other themes, ideas, and emotions seem insignificant. This seems to me an extraordinarily misplaced and even pernicious response, but it is nonetheless sufficiently seductive and widespread to require conscious resistance. Norma Rosen's article, "The Second Life of Holocaust Imagery," for example, is characteristic of this tendency. Rosen, who is not herself a camp survivor, insists that "for a mind engraved with the Holocaust, gas is always that gas. Shower means their shower. Ovens are those ovens. A train is a freight train crammed with suffocating children."[22] Although she qualifies this grisly description with the scarcely less overwrought acknowledgment that "of course this does not always happen. Some days the sky is simply blue and we do not wonder how a blue sky looked to those on their way to the crematoria,"[23] it is difficult to read the texture and rhetoric of the whole passage except as symptomatic of an almost clinically excessive identification with the suffering of others. One of the more enduring of the many horrors of the Shoah is that it seems to give such identifications the justification of a highly developed historical/moral imagination about the suffering of one's people. Dubious as I am about Fackenheim's notion of making certain one does not "grant Hitler a posthumous victory," if the phrase has any real meaning, I would argue that its import is not to tell people what kind of Jews they must now be, but rather to warn against regarding hallucinations like Rosen's as in any way a fitting memorial to the murdered.

No writer on the Shoah has been more aware of the risks of representing the ultimate viciousness of the Shoah, or more careful to avoid feeding an appetitive fascination with evil, than Aharon Appelfeld. A child of wealthy, thoroughly assimilated Bukovina Jews who were murdered in the Shoah, the nine-year-old Appelfeld survived by escaping alone from the Transnistria camp. Thereafter, he stayed alive by hiding in the forests and occasionally working for local peasants until the Russian army took him along as an assistant cook and helper in their sweep westward. Finally, he ended up in a refugee camp on the Italian coast, from which he was taken to Palestine by the Zionist youth rescue movement. Appelfeld, beyond any other prose writer, is credited in Israel with having made the Shoah into a legitimate theme for novelists. Writers like A. B. Yehoshua acknowledge that "Appelfeld . . . opened up new possibilities for treating the Holocaust in literature," and Yehoshua reminds us how much resistance Appelfeld's novels initially encountered among an Israeli public that, before the Eichmann trial, wanted to hear as little as possible about the world inhabited by the murdered Jews of Europe.[24] Central to the success of Appelfeld's writings has been the care he exercises in not allowing the violence of the killers to be directly represented in his novels. He has understood, as Henri Raczymow did not, that if one wants to avoid letting the details of Nazi savagery flood the narrative, then it makes little sense to allow one's gaze to approach right up to, but not enter, the gates of the death camps. From Appelfeld's perspective, the mass starvation, constant street murders, and beatings of the Warsaw Ghetto are as contaminated material as the gas chambers themselves, and in fact, there are hardly any Nazis in Appelfeld's books at all. His narratives of the Shoah take place among the secularized Jews of Austria and its eastern border states, and when the world of the surrounding Aryan majority is directly visualized, it is always in the form of peasants, minor officials, and morally compromised, but not blatantly sadistic fellow-townsmen, rather than through the typical bludgeon-wielding SS guards of Shoah exploitations.

Since I intend to criticize a constitutive, and in many ways ethically vitiating, weakness in Appelfeld's writings, it is only just also to acknowledge here that his accomplishment in legitimizing the Shoah as a theme for serious Israeli prose fiction is enormous. As Appelfeld noted in an interview, he began to write about the Shoah as a survivor-immigrant at a time when no one in his adopted country wanted to hear about the topic, in part as a willed decision of collective repression and in part because during the early years of statehood "personal experience was simply not worthy of recall. Only if you had been a pioneer . . . a partisan. Suffering by itself did not merit attention—unless it served a collective purpose."[25] (It is worth underscoring how different traditional Anglo-American criteria of judgments about literature are from those of Israel's pioneer generation of authors and readers. Until very recently, Western readers tended to cherish primarily, if not exclusively, the quality of personal experience and were suspicious of using that experience to serve a "collective purpose." But from the outset, and to an extent unimaginable in any other country, "Israeli Shoah literature . . . is *not* identified with first-hand testimony, with survivor's narratives.")[26] Appelfeld has been among the most prominent voices for a complaint common to many other immigrant-writers who share the sense that for a large number of Israeli Zionists, the entire experience of Diaspora Jewry, and even more so the Shoah, was a source of profound national embarrassment. Indeed, for many Israelis the culture that the survivors brought with them to Israel had no place in the new homeland.[27] For example, the Hungarian-born (1934), Israeli poet Itamar Yaoz-Kest describes having been treated as "the stooped, pale Gola Jew, a victim." He explains that "the condescending attitude of the Israeli towards the immigrant Jew is a direct offshoot of the revolt of Zionism against the Diaspora. The image of the Jew as victim is offensive and threatening to the Israeli ethos."[28] Nor can such a description be regarded as largely a projection of immigrant anxieties. In a meeting with Ben-Gurion, the poet and critic Leah Goldberg, herself an immigrant who only arrived in Tel Aviv from Lithuania in 1935, described survivors of the Shoah as "ugly, impoverished, morally suspect, and hard to love."[29] Since the Jews in Appelfeld's books are often unheroic, pale victims, morally suspect and extremely difficult to love, he ironically appears to have accepted the terms of the polemic in order to expose its logic, declaring himself the only author in Israel eager to be labeled "a 'Jewish' writer."[30] As Alan Mintz notes, "in an important sense, Appelfeld's rescue [from the Italian Displaced Persons' transit camp to Palestine in 1946] was a failure. As an orphan survivor, the boy was educated within the institutions of the Youth Aliyah [immigration] . . . movements; the ideological indoctrination these adolescents received encouraged them to disassociate themselves from the past: to forget it entirely and to make themselves over as Jews and as men in the image of the *sabra* [the tough, native-born, "new Jews" of the Zionist ideal]."[31] Tom Segev points out that "the task the country's leaders set for themselves was to give the survivors a new personality, to imbue them with new values. 'They must learn love of the homeland, a work ethic, and human morals,' said a Mapai [Israeli Labor Party] leader, and another one added that they should be given 'the first concepts of humanity.' One said, as if they were a huge ball of dough, that it was necessary to 'knead their countenances.' At one meeting of the Mapai secretariat it was said that they should be 're-educated.' "[32] Appelfeld's whole career has testified to just how determinedly he seemed to resist the pressures of that "re-education," and with what concentration he has included the European Jewish world he was taught to reject at the very center of his fiction.[33] This act of resistance required not merely great personal and imaginative integrity but also a kind of literary self-knowledge that, at its best, makes Appelfeld a crucial figure in contemporary writing per se, not merely in internal Israeli cultural and ideological debates.

Appelfeld's importance is centrally grounded in the fact that he is not only writing about the genocide as such, but rather, attempting to narrate the relationship between that catastrophe and the world it obliterated. But if the very act of representing European Jewry in its final months before the Shoah constituted both a thematic breakthrough and a polemical assertion of resistance in Israeli letters, the perspective from which Appelfeld treats his characters betrays an unconscious but thorough complicity with the sabras' contemptuous dismissal of the values and dignity of those Jews. There is a deeply troubling failure of historical and moral comprehension at the core of some of Appelfeld's most celebrated novels, and this failure is all the more disturbing since it is so strikingly at odds with the potential imaginative richness of Appelfeld's project as a whole. It is as though Appelfeld could only transgress the Israeli taboo against chronicling the unheroic lives of ordinary, assimilated Austro-German Jews, as well as the larger prohibition against any representation of the Shoah, by treating his characters as marionettes whose futile gestures on an absurd stage we watch, half in horror, half in anxiously bemused melancholy at their foolishness. We know they are doomed; they stubbornly refuse to know it, and in the interaction between our knowledge and their ignorance a fable of willed self-delusion unfolds whose motifs would have satisfied the strictest of Appelfeld's Zionist instructors in the youth movements.

I stress the element of "fable" in Appelfeld's narratives because this has been singled out repeatedly as praiseworthy by critics. By avoiding explicit reference to the Shoah, and more particularly, by refusing to allow the archetypal scenarios of concentration camp savagery to orchestrate the emotional force of his stories, Appelfeld succeeds in short-circuiting any possibility of the sadomasochistic identification that haunts literature on the Shoah. Similarly, whether triggered by the image of Hitler himself or by one of his stand-ins, ranging from Eichmann or Mengele to the unnamed but all-powerful SS thugs, the hypnotic fascination with pure evil can find no foothold in Appelfeld's books, focused as these are on the intricacies of Jewish self-delusion, class snobbism, and racial (self-)contempt. Robert Alter, in a review of *To the Land of the Cattails* (1986), notes that Appelfeld's "habitual strategy as a writer haunted by the Holocaust is to concentrate on its historical margins, either prelude or aftermath," and praises his "art of intimation" for rendering the terror of the Shoah "more powerfully than any direct introduction of violence."[34] An "art of intimation" is exactly the right phrase to define Appelfeld's characteristic procedure, but this art is purchased at the price of a psychological reductiveness and a historical flattening that ultimately may not be much preferable to the lurid repertoire of horror scenes it was intended to replace.

The best way to illustrate the cost of Appelfeld's technique is to look closely at *Badenheim 1939,* the first and critically most acclaimed of his novels to have appeared in English. (The Hebrew title, *Badenhaym 'Ir Nofesh* [Badenheim, Holiday Resort], does not contain the inappropriate specificity of the year, which was added for the American translation.) Badenheim is a typical Austrian spa town, where prosperous, thoroughly secularized Jews spend their vacations enjoying the restorative mineral baths, the rich hotel food, and the cultural life of an annual music and theatrical summer festival. In the novel, the town becomes a microcosm of the world of Austro-German Jewry with its cultural pretensions, its rejection of any overt signs of Jewishness, especially as embodied by the "vulgar *Ostjuden*" (Jews from Eastern Europe, whose style of dress, language, and religious observance exacerbated the unease of westernized Jews),[35] and its hallucinatory refusal to confront the danger that was literally enclosing it from every side.[36] Already a modern, if still unacknowledged, ghetto, Badenheim, in the course of the novel, is turned into a Third Reich transit camp by a series of ever-tightening legal restrictions imposed by the governing "Sanitation Department," until eventually, the final directive for a compulsory "resettlement" to the East orders the entire population to the railway station where "an engine coupled to four filthy freight cars" emerges to take them to their destination.[37] Even at the end, although the Jews of Badenheim have been deprived of their freedom, their jobs, and their contact with the outside world, and have been ordered about like so much chattel (but without any overt physical coercion, which would violate the book's fable-like tone), they retain their by now clearly absurd optimism. Dr. Pappenheim, a renowned impresario and musical connoisseur, and the most fully described character in the book, ends *Badenheim 1939* with the cheerfully encouraging comment, "If the coaches are so dirty it must mean that we have not far to go" (148).

But every reader of the novel knows the names of the stations where the train will disgorge its passengers, and if Appelfeld can avoid

mentioning Theresienstadt, Auschwitz, or Mauthausen, it is only because of his certainty that the reader will do so in his place. The
reader hears the desperate will to lie to oneself in Pappenheim's final
words and understands how soon and how methodically that Pan-
glossian confidence will be silenced. And what is of crucial importance, the reader understands this precisely from a deep familiarity
with the kinds of Shoah texts and images Appelfeld is applauded for
having excluded, so that in a sense everything that Appelfeld formally
bars from his fictional world he invites back in by virtually compelling
his readers to stage the horrific set-pieces in their own imaginations.
Ultimately, there is less difference than either Appelfeld or his admirers would like to claim between a concluding sentence like "If
the coaches are so dirty it must mean that we have not far to go" and
Pawel's "in the not too distant Austrian town of Braunau, one Clara
née Plözl, wife of the customs inspector Aloïs Hitler, had given birth
to . . . a sickly infant whose survival seemed doubtful. He survived."
Badenheim 1939 is so confident of its reader's familiarity with descriptions of Nazi bestialities that it never needs to mention them at all in
order to have their specter loom in the interstices of every scene and
dialogue. Thus, when Gabriel Josipovici interprets Appelfeld's "silence" about the camps as an implicit "condemnation" of writers
who "mythologize" the Shoah and whose texts feed our horrified
fascination with the details of the extermination process, he pin-
points the finest impulse in the novels but ignores the extent to which
their power is only made possible by the popularity of all the narratives Appelfeld's restraint is supposed to rebuke.[38] It is primarily with
these texts and images that *Badenheim 1939* is in dialogue, and what
is lost thereby is the reality of Austro-German Jewish life, as well as
an acknowledgment of the individual complexity on which genuine
understanding depends.[39]

Thomas Flanagan, in one of the best of the book's many laudatory
reviews, has described the atmosphere of *Badenheim 1939* as one of
"mild skies, strawberry tarts and fragments of idle conversation, the
weather of European social comedy. . . . At times . . . the novella
seems a pastiche of dozens we have read—cool, shapely comedies of
life in a genteel resort."[40] Flanagan's link of *Badenheim 1939* to con-

ventional social satires seems to me much more accurate than the often invoked parallel with Thomas Mann's *Magic Mountain*.[41] Both Mann and Appelfeld use resort settings as microcosms of a spiritually and politically diseased society, but Mann's characters are intensely aware of their predicament, and their conversations obsessively seek to diagnose that crisis. Appelfeld's vacationers just as obsessively deny that anything is wrong at all, and their conversations scarcely ever exceed the limited self-awareness typical of a comedy of manners. What Appelfeld has done, and it is a stylistically masterful decision, is to use the tonal resources of conventional summer resort comedies to construct an allegory of European Jewry on the eve of its annihilation. But as in the more typical of such mild satires, Appelfeld's tonal decisions make it impossible to take seriously the banal struggles and love affairs, indeed the entire inner world of his puppets, so that ultimately, the reader's shock at the gulf between the triviality of the characters' existence "on stage" and the gravity of the torment that awaits them after the curtain has set generates the only powerful emotion of the book.[42]

The expected, or, more accurately, the *necessary* importation of our knowledge about the Shoah is a particularly manipulative example of backshadowing because it seems so unemphatic and "natural." Moreover, it harmonizes perfectly with the tone of distant and aloof mockery used to describe the characters and their determinedly blinkered concentration on the quotidian banalities of resort life. But such an account of European Jewry only makes sense as a kind of *reductio ad absurdum* of the Zionist interpretation of Austro-Hungarian Jews stumbling blindly to their doom, willfully ignoring ever-clearer warning signs of the untenability of their position, and concerned only to distance themselves as much as possible from any acknowledgment of a common Jewish identity. (Leo Strauss used to call such rhetoric *reductio ad Hitlerum.*) Nothing can break through the triviality of the vacationers' narrow egotism, and when they leave for the railway station and its "four filthy freight cars," it is not a real existence that has been terminated, but only a sham construct with no more substance than the elaborate pastries of the Badenheim *Konditorei.* Appelfeld's fable, for all its seeming lightness of touch, is as moralistic and judgmental as the sternest critic of Austro-German Jewry, and, just as with all backshadowing perspectives, its termination in the abyss of the Shoah is adduced to "prove" the meaninglessness of Jewish life in Aryan Europe.

Badenheim's air of unreality is deliberately maintained throughout the book: from the pharmacist's garden, Pappenheim and his musicians "looked like a mirage" (9); the inspectors from the Sanitation Department seemed like "marionettes in a play" (11); from the railway station the deportees "could see ... the roofs of the houses like little pieces of folded cardboard" (145).[43] But the holiday atmosphere of this cardboard theater is, from the very beginning, traversed by flashes of fear, hysteria, and eventually even suicide, without the characters having sufficient consciousness to realize that their story has switched registers and that they have been uprooted into an entirely different genre. Their obliviousness is the novel's final judgment on the Jews of Badenheim and by extension, on Austro-German Jewry as a whole, who went, to use the part-embarrassed, part-contemptuous phrase of Zionist rhetoric, *Katso'n latevah* (like sheep to the slaughter). The knowledge, shared by the author and his readers, of what will befall the Jews of Badenheim becomes disturbingly self-congratulatory, harsh as this description may seem, primarily because life finds it extraordinarily hard not to be on the side of life, and when we read a book like *Badenheim 1939* or *The Retreat,* we are likely to be at least as angry at, as we are grieved by, the blindness of the characters. The fact that the historical consequence of the characters' blindness was death only makes the novelist (and hence the reader) more impatient with them and, drawing on the hollow wisdom of backshadowing, we are always able to tell ourselves that we would never have uttered such self-degrading assimilationist nonsense, that we would have been alert enough to flee in time, and that if we had been caught we would have resisted by any means available.

Other writers like Stefan Zweig and George Clare have described the quiescence of assimilated Viennese Jews, which continued even after Germany began to issue the Nuremberg decrees that stripped Jews of their citizenship and banned them from public life. Zweig describes the reaction of the majority of his acquaintances to the new racial laws being passed in Germany in the following terms: "Not even the Jews worried, and they acted as if the cancelling of all the rights of physicians, lawyers, scholars, and actors was happening in China instead of across the border three hours away, where their own language was spoken. They rested comfortably in their homes, rode about in their cars. Moreover, everybody had a ready-made phrase: 'That cannot last long.' "[44] Clare's equally striking account of Jewish self-delusion is set in Austria's most famous resort town, Bad Ischl: "Less than eight months later we were proscribed, hunted, despised. But in August 1937 we sat cozily in that little inn chatting time away as if it were stretching before us endlessly and happily."[45] Clare stresses that the misplaced sense of security that helped doom so many Austrian Jews allowed his family to enjoy their resort vacation in 1937. But his passage, which initially seems like an exact historical instantiation of Appelfeld's fictional drama, indirectly highlights a crucial index of how reductive such a vision can be. No doubt there is a bitter truth in some of Appelfeld's diagnoses, but that truth is compromised by the insistent backshadowing and allegorization that marks virtually every scene of *Badenheim 1939*.[46]

In an earlier section, I praised works that let us hear with sympathy the reasonableness of those European Jews who made the fatally wrong guesses about their chances for a peaceful assimilation into Austro-German society. But as with all historical judgments, the crucial question is exactly when these optimistic projections constituted the bases for people's decisions. Although the precise date is subject to debate, there is little doubt that there came a time when such hopes ceased being reasonable and became, for whatever personal reasons, delusional, because it was no longer a question of some unspecified future peril, but of a pervasive and imminent threat happening all around. But by setting his novel when he does, Appelfeld effectively blocks any engagement with the question of a plausible versus a willfully blind Jewish misrecognition of their situation. The addition of "1939" to Appelfeld's original title is not only irritating but unnecessary, because it is clear that his novel has to take place after the German annexation of Austria in March 1938. Although Austrian anti-Semitism had been both widespread and politically pow-

erful, the systematic registration, physical segregation, and deportation of Austrian Jews was a direct consequence of their sudden sub-
jection to the Nuremberg decrees. Moreover, the *Anschluss* itself was
accompanied by outbreaks of intense, widespread, and public anti-
Semitic violence, as well as by official acts of terror aimed at the entire
Jewish community. Almost immediately after the *Anschluss*, the Germans appointed Adolf Eichmann to drive all Jews out of Austria by
any means possible. Austria's Jews quickly faced an official terror that,
along with the casual brutality of much of the population, made their
position considerably more precarious than that of the Jews still living
in Germany proper. So effective was Eichmann's technique that a
higher percentage of Austrian Jews emigrated, and hence survived
the Shoah, than did German Jews.[47] Hence, if the Badenheim vacationers, like the historical Clare family, might have stayed stubbornly
blind to their endangered position in 1937, after the *Anschluss* no
Austrian Jew could have entertained any more doubts that his life was
in peril. Nor could any of them have sounded like Dr. Pappenheim,
"cheerfully" answering the question, "What's happened this year?"
with the reply, "Nothing out of the ordinary" (5).

This temporal difference is critical for understanding one of Appelfeld's most important, but hitherto unremarked, techniques:
while he endows his characters with the false sense of security still
possible in the late days of the Schuschnigg government (Kurt von
Schuschnigg [1897–1977] was Chancellor of Austria from 1934 until
Hitler's troops marched into Austria unopposed in March 1938), the
actions of the novel require that state power already be exclusively in
the hands of a Nazi administration. This double horizon makes the
characters seem all the more foolish. For example, in one of the most
dubious of the novel's barely disguised appropriations of Shoah imagery, no one reacts with any surprise or fear when the Sanitation
Department "took measurements, put up fences . . . unloaded rolls
of barbed wire, [and] cement pillars" (15). To the vacationers these
implements, whose provenance in concentration camp literature
both the narrator and readers know far too well, are only "suggestive
of preparations for a public celebration" (15). *Badenheim 1939* col-
lapses two historically distinct time frames within the narrative, and

then adds a third and authoritative one from outside the tale by which the others can be judged. The first, from well before the beginning of the Austrian Republic in 1918 to the *Anschluss*, is the epoch of a perhaps unhealthy but still possible assimilationism, a time when a significant number of prosperous Austro-German Jews sought to eradicate any characteristics considered "typically Jewish" in themselves and to repudiate them when they were manifested by the dreaded *Ostjuden*. The second phase, begun immediately after the German annexation, involved a swiftly accelerating isolation of all Jews from the rest of society through expulsion from most professions and schools, and included a series of threatening restrictions that culminated in an enforced ghettoization, which itself served only as a temporary measure before the physical extermination in the camps began. Each step of this process had its own distinct temporal rhythm and daily routines, and certain as they were of the Nazis' hatred, the Jews at first could not conceive of the enormity of the horror that was being organized to liquidate them. The two principal epochs, although chronologically close, are quite different moments, both historically and psychologically; collapsing them makes utterly unbelievable the consciousness of Appelfeld's characters, because it endows them with expectations and reactions completely inappropriate to their new circumstances. Our own distance from the events tends to foreshorten and flatten out our sense of the past and thus makes less noticeable Appelfeld's blurring of distinct time periods. Finally, it is also our knowledge of the Shoah, a knowledge that the author and reader share but of which the characters are entirely ignorant, that provides the novel's third time frame. It is this additional knowledge that makes us read the references to familiar phases of the genocide as so sinister, like the repeated invocation of a "happy" journey to a new life in Poland, or the barbed wire and cement pillars as normal props of a "public festival," and there is something almost cruelly manipulative about the way Appelfeld's narrator calmly registers these horror-charged images just to trigger the reader's feeling of dread. Consider, for example, the way Poland is regularly mentioned with an entirely different resonance for the characters and the readers: for example, "In Poland everything was beautiful, everything

was interesting" (25); " 'It will be completely different [in Poland],'
said Pappenheim. 'You can't imagine how different it will be' " (90).
The irony here seems to me stunningly callous toward the vacationers
whose self-deception and blindness hardly merit this degree of mockery.

The allegory of *Badenheim 1939* is created by making a single narrative out of the three temporal strands I have described, and for all
its tonal success, it is a deeply troubling strategy. The textual simul-
taneity of what were distinct historical moments saturates every novelistic element with too much, and sometimes contradictory, meaning, until the very excess of signification erases the book's grasp of
the real history of its story. We know, for example, that if Austria's
Jews wrongly trusted the Republic to protect them from the Nazis,
then as soon as that hope, along with the existence of Austria as an
independent nation, vanished, they hurled themselves at every possible foreign embassy trying, almost always in vain, to get a visa for
any other country.[48] The behavior of the vacationers in Badenheim
is not just blindly self-deceiving; it is also largely Appelfeld's own fantasy, belied by the pervasive terror that gripped Austrian Jewry within
hours of the *Anschluss*. The terror ended the era of fawning assimilationism Appelfeld satirizes,[49] and for all that epoch's miscalculations, class vanity, and even Jewish anti-Semitism, it merits a more
nuanced account than the mixture of psychological caricature and
chronological absurdity it receives in *Badenheim 1939*.

At its worst, an approach like Appelfeld's inadvertently makes the
issue of responsibility for the Shoah itself into a question. Saul Friedlander has highlighted a basic problem in many texts about the
Shoah: the risk that "the perpetrator's voice carries the full force of
aesthetic enticement; the victims carry only the horror and the
pity."[50] Appelfeld succeeds in avoiding this kind of "aesthetic enticement" by never mentioning the Nazis directly, but by representing
the Jews of Badenheim as irredeemably selfish and petty, he commits
the greater offense of leaving unchallenged the monstrous proposition that Europe's Jews are somehow "deserving" of punishment. As
Ruth Wisse points out, Appelfeld's allegory can only work by "taking
the real terror imposed from without by real human forces and in-

ternalizing it, thereby further obscuring its origins and meaning. . . . Fate sits in judgment on all the ugly, assimilated Jews—fate in the form of the Holocaust. The result is a series of pitiless moral fables more damning of the victims than of the crime perpetrated against them."[51] The result described here has nothing to do with Appelfeld's intention, but rather with the logical and rhetorical implications of his formal decisions and with the vision of history correlate with those decisions.

One way to crystallize the general implications of Appelfeld's practice in terms of my earlier discussion is to see how the "overdetermination" of signification forecloses any chance at sideshadowing. Since the relentless glare of the Shoah is ever present, not merely at the book's end but throughout its unfolding, it floods the various scenes with its overpowering significance so that none of them can have a consequence independent of that all-dominant one. Appelfeld himself clearly recognized the aesthetic and moral problem raised by backshadowing: his determination to avoid directly representing the Shoah by ending the novel before the killings actually began is part of this recognition. But since he never tries to voice an alternative and less monolithic vision of history, his novel incorporates none of the openness of sideshadowing, and his decision remains an isolated scruple unrelated to achieving a more complete understanding of the world of the victims.

Precisely this lack of penetration into the lived moral world and choices of Appelfeld's characters is why the effect of their inevitable, if only partially narrated, destruction at the end of *Badenheim 1939* differs so fundamentally from the equally foreseeable and calamitous fates of fictional figures like Hektor, King Lear, or Balzac's Lucien de Rubempré. There is a crucial and often unacknowledged distinction between the "inevitability" of an anticipated climax in classical epic and tragedy, or in densely "realistic" novels like those of the *Comédie humaine,* and the retrospective, backshadowing historico-moral judgments of a book like *Badenheim 1939.* In works like *The Iliad, King Lear,* or *Splendeurs et misères des courtisanes,* the grim ending is not used retroactively to constitute the primary source of judgment on the characters. What the characters in these works do is seen as

good or bad, evil or virtuous, at the moment their actions are committed. Lear is manifestly wrong and morally at fault right from his
first speech—even if Goneril and Regan had kept their pledges and
even if Cordelia were to have lived happily ever after in France, Lear's
tyrannical self-indulgence would be palpably reprehensible. But if
there had been no Shoah, the assimilationists vacationing in Badenheim might be considered, from certain perspectives, as weak or lacking in ethnic self-dignity, but from many other points of view, which
probably included those of the majority of European Jewry, their self-
definition as "Austrian citizens of Jewish origin" (21) would be entirely reasonable. To focus on one's private family ties, love affairs,
careers, or artistic longings, is completely unobjectionable by normal,
quotidian standards; only in the light of the genocide awaiting all of
the characters can these kinds of priorities be found inadequate. In
other words, the Shoah looming at the novel's end is used throughout the text, instant by instant and scene by scene, to judge everyone's
behavior, and it forces us to interpret that behavior as escapist, futile,
and ultimately self-destructive. This is not the case in a text, whether
epic, tragedy, or novel, whose ending, once it has occurred, may seem
retrospectively to have been predetermined but in which the episode-
by-episode, moment-by-moment behavior of the characters is significant in its own right. So, for example, Hektor may be doomed in the
judgment of the gods to die at the hands of Achilles, just as Achilles
in turn must die before Troy falls, but their decisions and deeds
throughout the poem have such resonance precisely because they
are shown to be of momentous significance to themselves, to their
companions, and even to the gods, irrespective of the end that awaits
both warriors.

It should be abundantly clear from this discussion that nothing in
my argument contests, let alone seeks to dismiss, the power of a literary tradition in which the audience's knowledge of the ultimate
destiny of the characters is a crucial component in a work's aesthetic,
emotional, and intellectual effect. But deterministic historical foreshadowing, unlike, say, classical tragic or heroic destiny, allows the
already known end to minimize, not intensify, the actual choices of
the characters, and it is as unlikely to succeed as are other attempts,

in a secular age, to substitute historicist patterns of inevitability for the certainties of a theological world view. In part, no doubt, back-shadowing often functions as our secular, historicist equivalent to the way a god can see the inevitability and interrelatedness of everything that happens. But in fact, stories about divine concern with the fate of time-bound mortals, whether set in the pagan world or in the Judeo-Christian one, with its insistence on the centrality of human "free will," make clear the importance of alternative choices in order to sustain any ethical judgment or even narrative interest. (Think, for example, of the story of Job, whose "test" depends entirely on the freedom that he does not exercise to curse God for the injustice of his sufferings.)

Of course my examples here are from works that we do not nec-essarily read for their historical specificity or analysis, but as I argued in my earlier discussion of Danto and Habermas, the ethical impli-cations of backshadowing are registered as powerfully in historical as in fictional writing. As we have seen, in a sense it is clear that without a knowledge of what followed them, it is impossible to grasp the sig-nificance and implications of decisive past events (e.g., the first anti-Semitic laws passed by the Nazis). But it is not the course of a partic-ular historical unfolding that is at issue here; rather, it is a respect for people living at a time *before* that unfolding was complete who could not, and should not, be expected to have any knowledge of the future. Sideshadowing is not concerned to deny to either the histo-rian or the novelist a retrospective awareness of important events; but it *is* concerned (1) not to regard the future from which the writers speak as the inevitable outcome of the past, and (2) not to let ret-rospection impose a hierarchy of significant/insignificant, fertile/futile, etc., judgments on the actions and thoughts of the characters in their narratives when the terms of that hierarchy are entirely de-termined by the story's ending.

But against my plea for the legitimacy of sideshadowing even in so unpromising a setting as Austria at the time of the *Anschluss,* it is understandably tempting to argue that "to speak of the dialectic be-tween freedom and necessity is to speak necessarily of a very one-sided dialectic."[52] Yet even at that moment in history there were other

choices in Austria than denial of the impending catastrophe, as numerous contemporary memoirs detailing the flood of Jews seeking
foreign visas makes clear. Even if most of the applicants were turned
away, the trapped Jews were unlikely to have chosen to continue visiting vacation spas in utter indifference to the network of exclusion-
ary and degrading legislation to which they were daily being made
subject. Even if some Austrian Jews did refuse to acknowledge their
perilous situation, the question of sideshadowing only indirectly concerns their likelihood of survival, which often was entirely out of their
own hands; instead, sideshadowing seeks only to draw attention to
the diversity of the stances they took toward their predicament and
the particular ways they sought to maintain their existence and identity within their catastrophic new circumstances. It is crucial to recognize that the likelihood of success of any action is not the criterion
by which a multiplicity of possibilities can be determined. Even if
none of the available options has a very strong chance of succeeding,
there are still differences among them (and since the issue here is
one of saving individual human lives, surely even a small percentage
is of enormous significance), and peoples' characters can be judged
partially by which option they in fact attempt. This is a position Appelfeld himself logically, if not in the actual texture of his narrative,
acknowledges, since otherwise he would not be able to ironize the
assimilationist Jews of Badenheim. Clearly, if there actually had been
no important individual choices left, then the Jews staying in places
like Badenheim acted in the only way they could and are inappropriate targets for satire; but if there had been numerous different
ways of reacting, as the historical record amply testifies, then Appelfeld's collapsing of the variety of Austro-German Jewish responses to
Nazism into a single, monological model is too reductive to constitute
a worthy or convincing satire.

   I am claiming here that to acknowledge the validity of sideshadowing is not merely to reject historical inevitability as a theoretical
model. Far more important, it means learning to value the contingencies and multiple paths leading from each concrete moment of
lived experience, and recognizing the importance of those moments
not for their place in an already determined larger pattern but as

significant in their own right. This is what I have called a prosaics of the quotidian, and it is fundamentally linked to the historical logic of sideshadowing. At a crucial point in *Badenheim 1939*, the narrator sardonically observes that "the people were still preoccupied with their own affairs—the guests with their pleasures and the townspeople with their troubles" (20).[53] This "preoccupation with their own affairs," as much as the denial of their Jewishness, is the unpardonable sin of everyone in Badenheim, and in Appelfeld's narrative it leads to consequences like the characters' general refusal even to discuss the fact that overnight "a barrier was placed at the entrance to the town. No one came in or went out" (38). Concern with the immediate and local, the familial and private, is judged inherently unworthy, an act of betrayal of others and of blindness to one's own deeper interests. Measured against the Shoah, as is everything in *Badenheim 1939*, Appelfeld's charge carries an intuitive plausibility, but it only makes sense if we agree to that standard of measurement; his scale loses its meaning if we consider, for example, that concern with one's ethnic identity, with the welfare of others in one's community, and with the nature of the political dispensation under which one lives, are themselves also local and personal matters, as much a part of prosaics as our "daily pleasures and troubles." In his contempt for prosaics, or, more accurately, in his linking of prosaics with pure selfishness, Appelfeld again rejoins the very ethos of the Israeli ideology that he thought he had rejected: "Personal experience was simply not worthy of recall. . . . Suffering by itself did not merit attention—unless it served a collective purpose." It is precisely distinctions like this that prosaics can not accept: a genuinely democratic, rather than a tyrannical, collective purpose can arise only out of the shared aims and hopes of the individuals who make up the larger group; such a purpose is the meeting point, not the liquidation, of the innumerable separate preoccupations and motives of everyone who agrees to work for the realization of the collective purpose.

Beneath the melancholy of its coolly appalled tone, the deeper irony of a work like *Badenheim 1939* is that while it finds a new idiom in which to narrate the margins of catastrophe, it also finds itself entrapped in the very explanations it deems unacceptable as soon as they are spelled out more clearly. Appelfeld himself has spoken with passion and sorrow about "this anti-Semitism directed at oneself. . . . Even after the Holocaust, Jews did not seem blameless in their own eyes. On the contrary, harsh comments were made by prominent Jews against the victims for not protecting themselves and fighting back."[54] (Appelfeld is presumably referring to Hannah Arendt, among others.) Although it is their assimilationism and lack of Jewish pride, not their inability to fight back, that is satirized, Appelfeld's characters collaborate so fully in their destruction that among those "prominent Jews" who make "harsh comments" about the victims of the Shoah, it is difficult not to include the author of *Badenheim 1939* himself. Even the most assimilated and self-denying Jews were still sufficiently Jewish to be murdered, and so the contempt of a novel like *Badenheim 1939* is just as "anti-Semitic" in its attribution of complicity as are the harshest judgments of the unnamed "prominent Jews."

What may seem like merely formal decisions about how much knowledge of the future to include in a narrative set in an earlier epoch, or about how much to let the narrative glance sideways and project forward to events that never happened, is already thematically charged and thereby morally significant. If it is absurd to see the "great world-historical event" of 1875 as Lenin's fifth birthday, and if we can smile at the idea of a secular angel arriving in Langres in 1713 to tell Mme. Diderot that she would soon give birth to a great encyclopedist, then we also have to learn to absolve from any blame those Jews who attended the summer festivals of Salzburg or Badenheim and went about dressed in *Trachten* rather than in the paramilitary gear of the *Haganah* or the *tephillin* of the orthodox. There is ample reason to find preposterous that it is now time to forgive the murderers. Recognizing the contingencies and uncertainties in human events can prevent us from blaming the victims for their disastrous choices, but it in no way mitigates the decisions and choices of their murderers. The consequences of evil actions may be unpredictable and continue long into the future, but they are committed by particular people at specific moments and can be recognized as evil as soon as they are performed. The murderers became such at the instant they participated in murder, and sideshadowing in no way minimizes—in fact, it only emphasizes—their moral culpability.[55] But enough time has passed for us to realize that it was always partially the shame of not having been there to help them survive that made blaming the victims of the Shoah so much a part of how the history of European Jewry has been figured since 1945. Sideshadowing eliminates neither historical responsibility nor moral judgment, but it insists we assign them prosaically: to individuals and individual actions where such judgments properly belong. It is these specific actions and choices made by individual people that constitute the history we inherit and with which our own actions and choices must ultimately come to terms.

4

BACKSHADOWING AND THE
RHETORIC OF VICTIMIZATION

Grief disappears, seriousness remains.
> Yitzhak Katzenelson, *Dos Lid Fun*
> *Oysgehargeten Yiddishen Folk*

If you could lick my heart, it would poison you.
> Itzhak ("Antek") Zuckermann to
> Claude Lanzmann in *Shoah*

Appelfeld's characters, whether the narratives in which they figure are set in pre-war Europe or in modern Israel, subvert the cardinal tenets of literary typology demanded by the theoreticians of sabra writing. Not only are the inhabitants of Appelfeld's fictional world unheroic, venal, and petty, but even the extremity of their suffering in the Shoah and the opportunities at self-transformation offered by a new Jewish state fail to ennoble them. In the despairing outcry of one of his most powerfully realized figures, the concentration camp survivor Bartfuss: " 'What have we Holocaust survivors done? Has our great experience changed us at all? . . . I expect'—Bartfuss raised his voice—'greatness of soul from people who underwent the Holocaust.' "[1] But "greatness of soul" is precisely what Appelfeld characters lack, and his suspiciousness of that entire category—especially of the claim that great agony must lead, in proportional response, to a compensatory greatness of inner development, is one of his true strengths as a writer. Alan Mintz usefully points out how Appelfeld's works set in contemporary Israel, with their cast of survivors who have reestablished lives as merchants, restaurant proprietors, and loan sharks "stretch the scope of classes and types [previously considered] deserving of the attention of serious literary art."[2] Mintz goes on to note that even those Israeli writers who rebelled against the demands of providing heroically "positive" models characteristic of the "generation of 1948" tended to draw their novelistic characters from the same social groups (kibbutz members, soldiers, teachers, writers) as had that first important generation of native-born Hebrew authors. They traced these characters' struggles entirely "within the institutional realities of the young state and . . . in reference to the faltering ideals of the socialist Zionist tradition." But Appelfeld refuses to represent his characters as anomalous within the new Jewish state. Rather, "the challenge of these stories to the values of Hebrew literature lies precisely in a normative claim: the State and all that it represents are, at some level, powerless in the face of other, prior realities."[3] Or, in Gershon Shaked's concise formulation: "In Appelfeld's works Hebrew literature becomes Jewish again, depicting *Jews* as persecuted victims; the Israeli romantic heroism only serves as an antithetical background."[4]

A remarkably pristine crystallization of the values of the 1948 or "Palmah" generation of Israeli novelists with which Appelfeld's concerns had to contend can be heard in the short story "The Sermon," by the Ukrainian-born Hebrew writer Haim Hazaz (1897–1973). The main character, Yudka, whose defining characteristic is a reluctance to speak in public, asks to deliver a statement before the committee of his kibbutz to discuss the school curriculum. At first Yudka has trouble articulating even the beginning of his idea, but then he gathers himself to declare, "I want to state . . . that I am opposed to Jewish history . . . because we didn't make our own history, the *goyim* made it for us. . . . What is there in it? Oppression, defamation, persecution, martyrdom. And again oppression, defamation, persecution, and martyrdom. And again and again and again, without end. . . . Just a collection of wounded, hunted, groaning, and wailing wretches always begging for mercy. . . . I would simply forbid teaching our children Jewish history. Why the devil teach them about their ancestors' shame? I would just say to them: 'Boys, from the day we were exiled from our land we've been a people without a history. Class dismissed. Go out and play football.' "[5]

It is impossible to mitigate the bitterness toward the entirety of Jewish Diaspora history in passages like Yudka's impassioned insistence that "Zionism and Judaism are not at all the same thing, but two things quite different from each other, and maybe even two things directly opposed to each other! . . . When a man can no longer be a Jew, he becomes a Zionist."[6] No doubt attitudes like Yudka's figured in the warning by even as passionate a Zionist as Gershom Scholem against the rejection of "Judaism" in Israeli ideology.[7] But a similar strain can be heard in thinkers both more sophisticated and less antagonistic toward the Jewish tradition than Hazaz. For example, Emil Fackenheim has referred to the sequence of events from the Shoah to the establishment of Israel as "the Jewish return to history."[8] Yet as Jonathan Boyarin is right to insist, "this is only true within a Hegelian conception of history as the history of states. If instead we view states as products of history, rather than the vehicle of history, it is altogether easy to see that Jews have been inextricably part of European and Mediterranean history for millennia."[9]

To Scholem, Jews have always been "in history," and the basic choice is whether to view Zionism in the way Yudka does, as the making of a totally new Jew, a "radical negation" of the past, free from an exile that brought only shame and weakness to Jews, or to conceive of it in the way Scholem himself did, as "a continuation and evolution of those forces that have determined the existence and endurance of the Jewish people even during the long years of dispersion."[10] The contemporary political sting to Scholem's question is to make one ask why and with what consequences it is *primarily* the history of anti-Semitic persecution and the fear of constantly new eruptions of the same disease that are still invoked by the Israeli right to legitimize the actions of the Jewish state rather than the historical values and traditions fundamental to Judaism itself. But well before statehood was achieved, Zionist leaders of every political orientation regularly invoked the rights conferred by Jewish victimization in their calculations. According to Shabtai Teveth, for example, by 1936 Ben-Gurion was maintaining that in the dispute between Arabs and Jews, their respective rights "would become functions of tragedies: the greater the tragedy, the greater the rights it conferred on its victims."[11] So it is scarcely surprising that early in 1992, a senior figure in what was then the Israeli government headed by Yitzhak Shamir said that any territorial negotiations were inherently suicidal because the pre-1967 borders of Israel were nothing but "the borders of Auschwitz."[12] Understanding the extraordinary pressures that this same cast of mind places on Israeli political discourse and self-conception helps to underscore the significance of the September 9, 1993 Israeli decision "to recognize the P.L.O. as the representative of the Palestinian people and commence negotiations with the P.L.O. within the Middle East peace process" (from the letter of Yitzhak Rabin, Prime Minister of Israel, to Yasir Arafat, Chairman of the P.L.O.).[13] The Israeli capacity to negotiate directly with the P.L.O. is part of a general loosening of both the claims and the anxieties of victimhood on the national imagination. As Yaron Ezrahi, an Israeli political theorist, remarks, "for years . . . Israeli leaders . . . drew from the Holocaust the pessimistic lesson that the only way Jews could survive in the post-Holocaust world, given the tragedy they experienced, was by relying on their swords. They can and should trust no one. No matter how strong Israel became, they always spoke and behaved like victims who had to be defensive and reactive. . . . What Rabin, who was the first Israeli-born Prime Minister . . . has done is draw just the opposite lesson from the Holocaust experience. . . . That lesson is that having power allows you to move in the direction of compromise."[14]

But deeper even than this crucial debate about the transformations of Zionism through the years of its struggle for statehood and politico-military power[15] is the whole question of how a people relate to their past, especially when that past is simultaneously so rich in accomplishment and so steeped in horror as that of the Jews. It is a question in which my theme of "foregone conclusions" is centrally implicated, because the very coherence of a sense of freedom depends upon how one understands one's relationship to temporality and succession. On a level that is simultaneously ethical and theological, I am haunted here by Walter Benjamin's paradoxical insistence that a significant existence need not imply either historical success or even the survival of one's works and name. What is at issue here, not only for Jews, but for anyone whose heritage has been brutally obliterated, is the ability to respond to and come to terms with that past without any sentimentalizing nostalgia. Instead, what is required is an awareness of the richness of historical moments whose potential has not been exhausted simply because they were defeated: "One might, for example, speak of an unforgettable life or moment even if all men had forgotten it. If the nature of such a life or moment required that it be unforgotten, that predicate would not imply a falsehood but merely a claim not fulfilled by men, and probably also a reference to a realm in which it *is* fulfilled: God's remembrance."[16] But even without invoking any transcendent restitution of obliterated possibilities, it remains true that learning how to live at once as self-shaping and yet in dialogue with one's history, both personal and cultural, is to understand the foundation in which the capacity to change, not just to repress, is grounded, a freedom in which creativity and necessity necessarily meet.

It is precisely this constantly metamorphosing recontextualization of memory, its location within both a historical continuum and a particular situation, that Appelfeld's writings so conspicuously lack, but which, ironically, is brought to them by the new historical experiences and concerns of their readers. A novel like *The Retreat,* for instance, which is an even harsher and historically more absurd allegory of the self-hating assimilationist drive of Austrian Jews, can be reread more disturbingly from an Israeli context as a critique of the "anti-Jewish" strain in Zionism itself. In *The Retreat,* a group of Viennese Jews has fled the decadent and viciously anti-Semitic capital, less to find refuge than to learn how to become more Aryan. They now try "assimilation into the countryside," in order to remake their weak, citified Jewish character (they describe themselves as "pampered, sensitive, slow, argumentative") into a new kind of being, by working the soil and getting closer to nature.[17] Their goal is "the kind of health which is conceivable only in people who work the land" (105). Their instructor, Balaban, "promised that within a short space of time he would painlessly eradicate embarrassing Jewish gestures and ugly accents" (62), and that strenuous manual labor and an avoidance of excessive intellectualization would finally heal the "sickly members of his race" (63). Of course this strategy utterly fails the refugees of *The Retreat,* much as in *Badenheim 1939* the fantasy that it still makes sense to call oneself "an Austrian citizen of Jewish origin" (21) is revealed as grotesquely self-deluding. What makes the historical/ethical perspective of *The Retreat* still stranger is that, unlike *Badenheim 1939,* it does recognize the intrinsic value of utterly prosaic, quotidian moments: making coffee, sharing food, and enjoying the warmth of a bed are celebrated, not scorned, in this book. The Jews of *The Retreat,* who arrive disliking one another and themselves, do learn to make a community and become connected to one another through their persecution and isolation. But crucially, they do not do so *as Jews.* Their new communitarian consciousness does not bring with it any change in their sense of what it means to be Jews— it is a totally atomistic transformation, occasioned by anti-Semitism but unconnected to a sense of specific cultural or historical options and decisions. (This fictional image is in striking contrast to the real situation in Austria, Germany, France, and Italy, where the enforced segregation of Jews and their expulsion from civil society brought with it a flowering of "returns" to Judaism and Jewish studies, especially among people who hitherto had shown no interest in Jewish culture.)

In *The Retreat,* the characters' slowly evolving respect for small, daily acts of mutual assistance and their growing personal courage seem particularly hollow because, in spite of their struggle to survive surrounded by racist enemies, nothing ever brings them to amend, or even to think about, their own Jewish self-hatred. In Appelfeld's novels, it is as though such self-hatred were simply a biological/historical "given" of assimilated European Jews, more fundamental to their natures than even the instinct for survival and unamenable to modification no matter what their actual circumstances. Ultimately, as still another variation on the Badenheim motif, *The Retreat* is interesting only as an example of how bitter and heavy-handed Appelfeld's allegories become without the devices of genteel social comedy to act as a tonal counterpoint to his theme. But reread against the grain of its own explicit intentions, *The Retreat* becomes fascinating for its insight into the pressure with which the sabras sought to remake the European survivor immigrants into new, physically tough, and manually dexterous Jews. For the *yishuv* (the Jewish community in Palestine before statehood), as Tom Segev insists, "negation of the Exile took the form of a deep contempt, and even disgust, for Jewish life in the Diaspora, particularly in Eastern Europe, which was characterized as degenerate, degraded, humiliating, and morally corrupt. In their tragedy, Diaspora Jews seemed even more repellent."[18] Berel Lang has also analyzed disturbing parallels between the Nazi rhetoric about Jews in general and certain left-wing Zionist descriptions of the assimilated Jewish bourgeoisie in the *Galut:* "the convergence of certain formulations . . . extends even to the use of common metaphors and in particular the charge against the Jews of the Diaspora of 'parasitism' . . . or of being 'diseased.' "[19] Perhaps the only truly frightening moments in *The Retreat* come when the reader begins to be haunted by the similarity among three converging tropes: the Jewish self-contempt expressed by Appelfeld's characters about themselves, the traditional rhetoric of Austrian anti-Semites, and the scorn voiced by Zionist polemicists against the characterless and deracinated Jews of the *Galut:* "But the Jews are rodents; not for nothing does the world regard them as animals of the rodent species. I myself . . . what was I all those years but a rodent?" (104–5).

I do not intend to propose an ironic new interpretation of *The Retreat* as a satire on the anti-Jewish strain in left Zionism,[20] potentially illuminating though that might prove, but to show how different contexts and circumstances provide a text with a penumbra of sideshadows that decisively inflect the ways it can be read. In this sense, parody can be considered an effect of sideshadowing, exposing as it does the partiality of any position that "ignores or claims to transcend its own originating context."[21] Because parody is most readily invited by doctrinal utterances that seek to present themselves as absolute, some recent Israeli novelists have been strongly attracted to showing how the Zionist prescriptions of the founder generation resonate differently in the nation today. For example, Meir Shalev's novel, *The Blue Mountain* (published in Hebrew in 1988; translated into English in 1991), contains a wonderfully comic metamorphosis of the Zionist injunction that the "normalization" of Jews could only take place through the redemption of the earth of *Eretz Israel* by physical labor. Set in a village in the Jezreel Valley, the novel is full of ironic side-shadowing, bringing to light consequences undreamed of by the heroic pioneer-ideologists. Among the most audacious of these ironies is the decision by one of the book's principal characters to turn his fruit and vegetable garden into a private cemetery. Still worse, he then charges outrageous sums to wealthy *Galut* Jews who had come to Palestine during the Second Aliyah (ca. 1904–14), then left when times became too hard, but still long to be buried back in the soil they deserted. When the village objects to this plan as violating everything for which the community has stood since its foundation ("We returned to the earth to farm it and to live by our own labors"), they are told by the narrator's lawyer, "My client is acting in perfect conformity with the ideals of cooperative farming. . . . My client is definitely engaged in returning Jews to the earth . . . [and] quite literally earns his livelihood from the earth."[22]

A novel like *Badenheim 1939*, of course, is completely devoid of sideshadows: its plot, characterization, and figuration are unswervingly single-minded, moving inevitably from the first sentences to the railway station and its "four filthy freight cars." But the contexts of pre-war Zionist polemics against the Diaspora and of post-war Israeli scorn for the weak, European Jew as a permanent victim in need of remaking, provide precisely the kind of new light in which a text like *The Retreat* acquires sideshadows that probably were never part of its author's intentions and that unwittingly bring it closer to the parodic element in a novel like *The Blue Mountain*.[23] Sideshadowing, then, can also be thought of as the entire set of alternative interpretations, subsidiary plots, and interrogations that history encourages us to add to a work by uncovering new connections, ramifications, or contradictions between it and the world of lived actuality. Without sideshadowing, the targets of a historical satire like *Badenheim 1939* are too clearly and immobilely in focus: there is no history because there is no process, only a totally static universe with unvarying global oppositions. This attempt to freeze history and reduce it to a set of immutable and strictly hierarchized binary categories (Aryan/Jew; healthy/degenerate; *Übermensch/ Untermensch;* party loyalist/enemy of the people; proletarian/bourgeois; revolutionary/reactionary; etc.) is characteristic of all totalitarian thinking, which, whether fascist, Nazi, or communist, is profoundly anti-historical and inimical to all forms of sideshadowing.

Irrespective of one's intentions, it is also impossible to contest any of these totalitarian ideologies coherently without at the same time rejecting the figurations through which they organize and explain the world. Just as the most solid objects look different under different angles of light or set among differently shaped shadows, the certainties of ideology are threatened by sideshadowing's emphasis on the nonsystematic and the accidental. If history, rather than being governed by the iron code or law claimed by various schools of "semiotic totalitarians,"[24] actually manifests a marked degree of unpredictability amid its changes, then the creation of new shadows and unexpected patterns will be unavoidable. After noting that "the Holocaust has already engendered more historical research than any single event in Jewish history," Yosef Hayim Yerushalmi goes on to speculate that there is "no doubt whatever that its image is being shaped, not at the historian's anvil, but in the novelist's crucible."[25] Although the responsibilities and the decorum of the two genres should never simply be collapsed together, neither is Yerushalmi's distinction between the historian and the novelist as absolute as his antithesis requires. In both kinds of writing, when the subject is an event as grievous as the Shoah, the carefulness of the imagination must accompany the carefulness with which the evidence is assembled and analyzed. Ultimately, it seems to me that the crucial issues have little to do with the differentiation in which Yerushalmi places his trust. What is needed, instead, is to challenge the fundamental narrative codes and interpretive strategies used to articulate the explanation of the world necessary for apocalyptic, Messianic history—a history of which the Shoah was the demonic counter-incarnation. A new kind of anti-totalitarian narrative is called for, in which a prosaic, quotidian voice can contest at the formal as well as the thematic level the absolutist ideology that makes mass murder conceivable. This is possible in both history and fiction, and perhaps equally difficult in both, precisely because each is so deeply penetrated by an ethos of the decisive and exceptional, and each is so accustomed to the claims of foreshadowing. The whole argument of my book rests upon the elemental premise that sideshadowing is an essential aspect of such a new, prosaic narrative. The historical understanding whose direct correlative is sideshadowing not only speaks for the possibility of an always open, always undetermined future but also looks back at the past with a solicitude for the world that was wiped out, for the possibilities it contained, and for the victims who once lived within the horizon of those now permanently obliterated but once real possibilities.

■   ■   ■

> And in each of these diverging stories all the others
> are reflected. . . . If . . . only one version . . . has come
> down to us, it is like a body without a shadow, and
> we must do our best to trace out that invisible shadow
> in our minds.
>
> Roberto Calasso,
> *The Marriage of Cadmus and Harmony*

> I think there are as many ways of surviving survival as
> there have been to survive.
>
> Philp K., quoted in *Holocaust Testimonies*

For centuries it was in large part through the common telling of its stories and the imaginative loyalties they fostered that Jewish survival was ensured. But the two enormous transformations of Jewish existence in this century—the Zionist movement and the establishment of the State of Israel on the one hand, and, on the other, the previously unimaginable horror of the Shoah—profoundly altered the patterns discovered in—or, as I have argued, imputed to—the narratives that are now constructed to articulate the meaning of Jewish histories. The kind of ameliorative "Whig Interpretation of History" against which Herbert Butterfield already warned in 1931 has reemerged in an inverted, daemonic version as a grid for reading European Jewish history, but it is one that has no more coherence or analytic rigor than optimistic historical master plots. To recapitulate my position in its most polemical formulation: I think that in the ways the history of European Jewry has usually been narrated, its annihilation in the camps is granted a kind of negative teleology that then retroactively provides the terms by which its entire experience prior to the Third Reich is judged. And as we have seen, backshadowing of this sort, whether in the melodramatic formulations of a Pawel or Berkeley, or in the elegiac ironies of an Appelfeld, inevitably denatures the very different possibilities facing Jews living at different historical moments, under radically incommensurate and often rapidly changing conditions. It has also made the Shoah the foundation for a certain kind of modern Judaism, in which the claims of victimhood as constitutive of Jewish experience throughout history are asserted either for their potent political charge or as cultural talismans to be celebrated or chafed against depending on the particular speaker's temperament and intentions.[26] Beyond the immediate political consequences of such a position, consequences that include, but are not limited to, an emotional/rhetorical climate in which successive Israeli administrations seek to mobilize Jewish loyalty through a calculated appeal to the same tragic story (i.e., "*Eretz Israel* as the last refuge of the [inevitably persecuted] Jews"), there is a more insidious corollary to privileging the Shoah in such a way. Whether unwittingly, or as part of an explicitly accepted belief, each time the Shoah is evoked in the terms I have described, it relies on the logically prior assumption that the real "proof" of the worth of an individual, a doctrine, or a political/ethical system is how it holds up under the harshest testing imaginable—a kind of *in extremis veritas* interpretation of an entire culture and all of its specific practices.

Clearly nothing of what I have written should be taken as an attempt to disparage the ongoing studies of the historical roots, political context, and (if this is the right phrase) bureaucratic "institutionalization" of the Shoah. But analysts are right to underline that Menahem Begin was the first Israeli Prime Minister regularly to invoke the Shoah in his major addresses, and anyone fascinated by the evocative power of narrative and rhetorical patterns will register how fraught with risks such a backward glance can be when it encourages, implicitly or by design, apocalyptic fears through the medium of its evocations. As we can see today both in Israel and in the American political and academic body, once victimhood is understood to endow one with special claims and rights, the scramble to attain that designation for one's own interest group is as heated as any other race for legitimacy and power. Victimhood, one needs to remember, is scarcely a fixed term, and there is something truly depressing in the clamor of competing voices to prove whose distress has been more persistent and devastating, and whose claims to compensatory rectification are therefore more worthy. For a particularly demoralizing example of this tendency one need look no further than the August 1991 Crown Heights turmoil between the Lubavitcher and the black communities and the ways in which it was immediately inscribed within competing narratives of victimization. Long infuriated by the perceived special treatment accorded to the Lubavitchers, black anger was triggered when a car in the Grand Rebbe's entourage jumped a curb and struck two black children, killing one, Gavin Cato, and seriously injuring his cousin, Angela. In the three days of riots that ensued, a twenty-nine-year-old Australian Jewish scholar, Yankel Rosenbaum, was murdered and two more Hasidic men were stabbed. The assaults were accompanied by intense anti-Semitic harassment in which Jews were compared to slave owners and the death of Cato was seen as a direct continuation of the callous disregard for black lives on the slave ships and plantations. In an article revealingly entitled "Invisible Man: The Lynching of Yankel Rosenbaum," David Evanier recounts how "the media at best treated the accidental death of Gavin Cato and the murder of Rosenbaum as morally equivalent. The worst ignored Rosenbaum entirely. The conflict between blacks and Jews was seen as being in balance, with the 'social justice' edge going to the blacks. . . . Anti-Semitism was not mentioned in any editorial about Crown Heights in New York newspapers until August 29 [nine days after the killing] in the *New York Post.*"[27] But even though Evanier's accusation of moral obtuseness on the part of the New York media seems to me in the main justified, his own narrative is itself decidedly problematic. The reason the media tended to see "the 'social justice' edge going to the blacks" was primarily because in the United States, Jews are not regarded as a vulnerable minority, while

African Americans are perceived, both rhetorically and legally, in such terms. But instead of contesting the whole ideology of justification by degree of historical victimization, Evanier, as the title of his piece clearly announces, wants only to reassign the status of principal victim, first by casting Yankel Rosenbaum as the 1991 equivalent of the unnamed black narrator of Ralph Ellison's *Invisible Man,* and then by claiming that the Lubavitchers today run as great a risk of public lynchings as did Southern blacks during the Jim Crow era. The Lubavitcher community itself, in the form of the "Crown Heights Emergency Fund," placed a full-page advertisement in *The New York Times* on September 20, 1991, under the heading "This Year Kristallnacht Took Place on August 19th Right Here in Crown Heights." Their version of Leo Strauss's *reductio ad Hitlerum* was rightly perceived by those who had been in Germany on *Kristallnacht* (November 9, 1938) as an outrageous comparison. The brutal beatings and mass arrests of thousands of Jews, the looting of Jewish homes and stores throughout the country, and the burning of Jewish synagogues, libraries, and community centers, all organized and planned by the state itself, simply bears no relationship to the events in Brooklyn.[28] However, I am not concerned here to reexamine the circumstances leading to the death of Gavin Cato and the murder of Yankel Rosenbaum, but rather to question the entire urge to establish one's credentials as an eternal victim in order to claim an unassailable moral high ground. Such a claim could only be substantiated by interpreting each unhappy event as a repetition/continuation of the worst experiences in the communal memory, with the result that it almost seemed to both sides to have been Nazis and slaveholders who confronted one another, rather than citizens of Brooklyn in 1991.[29] Were the consequences of such distortions not so pernicious, they might almost be comic: the image of a Southern plantation owner with *peyas* (sidelocks), dressed in a Hasidic black coat and wearing his *tallit* and *tephillin* (prayer shawl and phylacteries) confronting a black dressed in the SS regalia of the Aryan master race has an undeniably macabre absurdity to it.

Moreover, as my examples make clear, in spite of current assumptions in this country, to criticize the rhetoric of victimhood does not mean aligning oneself with any particular political party or direction. Throughout much of this century in Europe, the primary political expression of the sense of being injured, and of anger at having been reduced to the role of a marginalized victim, has been the province of the far right. Fascism and Nazism both capitalized on and fueled the ressentiment of people who were convinced that they had been unfairly mistreated, while others (usually the Jews, but also intellectuals, homosexuals, members of Masonic lodges, etc.) had received unmerited privileges. Hitler, in particular, regularly appealed to the Germans to see themselves as innocent victims of a host of interlocked evils ranging from the Versailles treaty to parliamentary corruption, all secretly orchestrated by an international Jewish conspiracy intent on world rule. Insofar as the increasingly problematic categories of "left" and "right" still retain any useful meaning today, it is instructive to see that the position of justification by one's historical affliction is invoked in Israel largely by the political and cultural right, while in North America and the United Kingdom this is done primarily by the left. Yet people who are quite willing to resist the Likud Party's invocation of the Shoah to legitimize its policies are swayed by analogous arguments derived from the horrors of slavery, or the history of gender, race, and sexual-orientation–based discrimination and violence, in order to justify the creation of a newly ennobled victim group whose refrains of oppression are manipulated for legislative and political ends.[30]

It took considerable courage for the Israeli novelist A. B. Yehoshua to remind a predominantly Jewish readership that "we must bear in mind that our having been victims does not accord us any special moral standing. The victim does not become virtuous for having been a victim. Although the Holocaust inflicted a horrible injustice upon us, it did not grant us a certificate of everlasting righteousness. The murderers were amoral; the victims were not made moral. To be moral you must behave ethically. The test of that is daily and constant."[31] This same distinction holds true, unpopular though such a view is, for victims of AIDS, racism, rape, or cancer, or any of the numerous brutalities and inequities that continue to flourish in our society. Indeed, it seems to me an indecency to assume that victims are somehow "ennobled" by their (usually involuntarily undergone) suffering, since such an assumption necessarily endows the cause of the suffering with the capacity to bring out a previously hidden worthiness. If anything, as the experience of recent history has shown, too sharp a sense of one's own victimization can easily lead to a compensatory urge to tyrannize over others, and those convinced of their unique victimhood are quite likely to prove tyrants both to themselves and to others if given the chance, whether their frustration is confined to a protest against the curriculum in a modern university, expressed in the mob violence of an urban riot,[32] or vented in the murderous rampage of Baruch Goldstein, whose killing of at least forty unarmed Muslims was cheered by many of his fellow *Gush Emunim* settlers on the West Bank.[33]

For Jewish thought, what is most troubling in the conjunction of foreshadowing and the sense of victimization in narratives like Appelfeld's or Pawel's is its complicity with the dispiriting cliché that sees the entirety of Jewish existence as nothing more than a wrenching from horror to horror. It is exactly against what Salò Baron called this "lachrymose view of Jewish history" as only a *Jammergeschichte,* an endless tale of woe, that the best volumes of modern Jewish historical and cultural studies have been written, studies as diverse in scope and methodology as Baron's own *Social and Religious History of the Jews* and Gershom Scholem's re-creation of Jewish kabbalistic and mystical thought. In a crucial essay entitled "Deformations of the Holocaust," Robert Alter urged that "it is as important to study how the Jews *lived* as how they died."[34] In many ways, I believe that it is Alter's formulation, with its principled refusal to interpret the Shoah as the single defining event of Diaspora Jewish history, rather than Fackenheim's 614th commandment, that offers a more productive relationship to the achievements, as well as to the pain, of the past two millennia of Jewish experience.

But just as important, I want to insist that *any* sense of identity as constituted primarily by victimization is an extraordinarily problematic basis for either an individual or a group to build upon, and the sad truth is that, in contrast to the celebrated opening of Tolstoy's *Anna Karenina,* it is "unhappy" consciousnesses that so much resemble one another in their misery, while happiness is always singular and hard-won. More challengingly, though, and against much of the writing done today on the Shoah from both religious and philosophical perspectives, I believe that very little about human nature or values can be learned from a situation *in extremis* except the virtual tautology that extreme pressure brings out extreme and extremely diverse behavior. Beliefs, ideas, values, and people are tested best in the daily, routine actions and habits of normal life, not in moments of extraordinary crisis, and because foreshadowing can only point to a single, inherently dramatic, rather than typical and quotidian resolution, it must privilege the uniquely climactic over the normative and repeatable. To reject the validating force of extreme crises involves both formal and ethical decisions precisely because such a rejection, based as it is on a moral stance, necessitates finding a new form of writing in order to articulate its new understanding. And only a prosaics of sideshadowing can, I think, do justice to the richness, both humanly and philosophically, of the claims of the ordinary, because it recognizes how various the strands of that ordinariness really are and how shrilly thin by comparison are the dramas we usually take as revelatory.

For someone who has been through the bleakness of the concentration camps, the conviction that the experiences undergone there have revealed a fundamental truth about the world often seems irresistible. Thus, Irene W., one of the survivors whose videotaped interview Langer cites, explains that the "extreme pessimism" that haunts her is part of a "total worldview" in which she feels that she has learned the real "truth about people, human nature, about death . . . [I emerged] knowing the truth in a way that other people don't."[35] A member of my own family who was interned in Sachsenhausen as a youth before being permitted to leave for England still finds it difficult not to take the world of the camps as a kind of ultimate criterion by which to evaluate both his own subsequent experiences and the actions of other people. We need to be extraordinarily careful neither to condemn survivors for the bitterness that they insist is only the "truth" the rest of us are too sheltered or afraid to acknowledge, nor to share their judgment in our own thinking.

For many, but by no means all survivors, their time in the camps *is* the central truth of their lives and stays with them, in Langer's phrase, like "a communal wound that cannot heal."[36] We need to respect their "total worldview," but it is not, nor should we try to make it, the truth of ours. Even Primo Levi, whose best writing continually returns to reevaluate and reanalyze his experiences in Auschwitz, refuses to think of the concentration camp as a uniquely privileged source of insight into human nature. To the question whether "it is necessary or good to retain any memory of this exceptional human state (questa eccezionale condizione umana)," Levi answers in the affirmative, but only because he is certain "that no human experience is without meaning or unworthy of analysis, and that fundamental values, even if they are not positive, can be deduced from this particular world (questo particolare mondo) which we are describing."[37] It is worth lingering here to register just how carefully Levi reverses customary judgments about the camps. If the by-now conventional claim is that Auschwitz, because of its brutality and ruthlessness, represents a uniquely authoritative testing place of human beings, Levi implies that its exceptional nature actually makes the Lager unreliable as a "laboratory." It is the *singularity* of the Lagers, not their representative or emblematic character, that Levi shows we need to keep clearly in focus, especially now that the Shoah is invoked so often to substantiate and lend emotional force to a diffuse range of arguments about modern society, fundamental human nature, or the character of Western culture as a whole.

In spite of the impassioned self-identification with and search for an absolute (even though absolutely negative) meaning in the experience of the Shoah by writers like Norma Rosen or Cynthia Ozick, no one becomes a survivor either by virtue of being a Jew or by the intensity of their absorption in the history and literature of the Shoah (e.g., Sylvia Plath's notorious lines from "Daddy" : "An engine, an engine / Chuffing me off like a Jew. / A Jew to Dachau, Auschwitz, Belsen. / I began to talk like a Jew. / I think I may well be a Jew.").[38] This fact needs to be emphasized because it can serve as a corrective to an unconscious, but therefore all the more insidious, "idealizing" (in the sense of "taking as a globally instructive model") of the

Shoah. Because so much of our culture is still strongly bound to the belief that the truth lies in the extreme moments which "ordinary bourgeois life" covers over and that it is only at the (appropriately named) "cutting edge" of the unthinkable that the most valuable insights lie hidden, it has become possible, by a truly grotesque inversion, to interpret the ruthlessness of the Shoah as offering the most authentic—because most horrendous—image of the underlying reality of our world. Although the extent, brutality, and single-mindedness of the Nazi genocide are unprecedented, its narrative incorporation into what one can call an ideology of the extreme has the paradoxical, and entirely unintended effect of assimilating it to a cultural tradition that itself encouraged a turn to the excessive and the apocalyptic. (Notice here, as well, how this paradox, in which the genocide is simultaneously regarded as utterly unique and yet emblematic of the modern world, perfectly recapitulates the earlier contradiction I have discussed between the Shoah interpreted as at once unimaginable and inevitable.)

The fascination with the brutal and the dangerous holds a compelling place in our culture's imagination. In Joseph Conrad's *Lord Jim*, for example, the narrator, Marlow, tells his listeners that "the truth can be wrung out of us only by some cruel . . . catastrophe," and Jim himself is advised that the only way to test himself is by seeking out the most extreme and trying circumstances possible: "To the destructive element submit yourself. . . . In the destructive element immerse."[39] But, as Dostoevsky had already predicted at the end of the nineteenth century, it is not that far from the celebration of authenticity, risk, and spontaneity to envisaging murder as the final and potentially most purifying confrontation with "the destructive element" in humankind. Moreover, as Sidra DeKoven Ezrahi points out, it is Jewish culture that regularly has been "decimated by the apocalyptic fantasies of others,"[40] and in the refiguring of the extermination of European Jewry it is especially important not to allow an internalized version of that same imaginative legacy to dictate the terms within which the Shoah is interpreted.

There is a subtle but clear link between the view that the truth stands out most clearly in an extreme situation and the conviction

that a hidden system or pattern exists waiting to be uncovered beneath the diversity of normal human existence. Both attitudes long
for global revelations and are contemptuous of "mere" contingencies. Both are in quest of a revelatory moment that will disclose the
one truth that matters, whether that moment be one of interpretive
acumen (e.g., Freud's description of himself as a heroic *conquistador*)
or of extreme physical risk (e.g., the glorification of the battlefield
as an arena of personal revelation). Against this notion of truth being
found at the utmost hazard of life, the prosaics of sideshadowing
wants to locate it in the ordinary and quotidian actions of our communal existence. To grasp just how provocative this proposition really
is, it is worth emphasizing that sideshadowing's critique of "semiotic
totalitarianism" applies with equal force both to the interpretive
model of the human psyche proposed by the reductionist strain in
psychoanalysis as well as to Tolstoy's character Pierre Bezukhov's trust
in the Masonic mysteries in *War and Peace;* it encourages the same
skepticism toward Hegelian or Marxist teleological readings of history
as it does toward earlier master tropes like chiliastic numerology.
Sideshadowing is defined by its attention to the pressures of randomness and contingency, to a view of the self as an aggregate of ever-
changing habits, memories, and experiences, shaped in part by un-
foreseen and unforeseeable circumstances, and to a notion of truth
as precisely what is *not* a puzzle to be solved or a revelation to be
authenticated in a unique climactic struggle. Hence, too, prosaics
insists on an understanding of time as a succession of content-rich
differences, rather than as an endless repetition of identically meaningless units suddenly punctuated and redeemed by the thunderclap
of the cataclysmically significant crisis. As Berel Lang argues, "a math-
ematical proof demonstrates no more in its second or third repetition
than it did the first time—and moral judgment differs from theoretical reason in just this respect, that as it faces the 'same' issue again,
it may incorporate that new judgment into the past. . . . Time appears
an intrinsic element of moral judgment."[41] But, as Lang's own uneasy
quotation marks are designed to show, in human experience neither
the issues nor the people confronting them are ever really "the

same," so that an attentiveness to temporality and a recognition of the differences it entails are not just one part of, but an indispensable foundation of moral judgment.

Similarly, because it is so dismissive of temporal development and historical context, any ideology that endows victimhood with a singular authority to make claims upon others who were not themselves the agents of the injury, strikes me as morally incoherent. Prosaics, with its emphasis on the incommensurability of specific moments, and sideshadowing, with its commitment to the multiplicity of paths issuing out of each of those moments, necessarily resist such an ideology. For a prosaics of sideshadowing, the question of how to live one's ethnic, racial, or sexual heritage is a subset of the more general issue of finding a proper relationship to temporality and communal identity. Against current ideologies that compete about which one of these aspects, most commonly either the ethnic or the sexual, should be seen as somehow foundational for the entirety of one's being, prosaics regards each one as an equally valid ground base upon which one learns to play out the infinitely complex variations that constitute our freedom. Bakhtin would argue that counterlives are imaginatively enriching because, to adapt Caryl Emerson's apt phrase, they remind us of the primacy of the differences we *make* over those with which we are born.[42] As a corollary to this theme one can add Michael Frayn's insistence that "we don't choose a moral response [from a pre-established set of options], we construct one."[43] The step-by-step, never-identical construction of a life, a history, and an ethic is the core of a prosaic practice and the principal imaginative lesson of sideshadowing.

In Jewish thought, the privileging of the claims of victimhood has created what Michael R. Marrus calls "the triumphalism of pain,"[44] but versions of that triumphalism flourish throughout Western society, operating simultaneously at the level of high art, mass culture, and political rhetoric. Frayn shrewdly asks why the paradigm of literature should so closely resemble a kind of *Consumer's Report* description of a new product: "Like electric toasters, the characters of fiction are tested, by stress and crisis, until they break down. And the convention is that what emerges at this point is their 'real' nature, which has up till then remained hidden from others and even from the owners of the nature themselves.''[45] The strength of this paradigm is evident throughout our culture, not merely in literature, and its persistence testifies to the interpenetration of tropes from one register to another. If the narration of Jewish history has any generalizable lesson, it is surely to illustrate the dangers of such a convention. The fact that Jews, as often as anyone else, lay claim in their own self-interest to a special access to truth derived from their unprecedented suffering only shows the persistence of a cultural topos even among those who, in other ways, have sought strenuously to shed the role. More generally, because the Shoah has been appropriated so often during the past four decades as an all too available archetype of both personal and collective suffering, its meaning has been assimilated to the most conventional données of our epoch. Despite the ritual insistence on the singularity of the genocide, the "final solution" has itself become one of the most often adduced instantiations of an unexamined and deeply false commonplace—the belief that the real worth of our culture can only be authoritatively tested at the extreme limit of human behavior.

" 'For example' is no proof,'' runs a Yiddish proverb. Perhaps there are no proofs, only examples, each one an intricate reality of its own, linked to the others but containing a rich repertoire of counterlives and sideshadows that we are only beginning, in the face of deeply entrenched conventions, to value for their very resistance to the demand for a final proof.

5

SIDESHADOWING AND
THE PRINCIPLE OF THE
INSUFFICIENT CAUSE

One had an impression of a process of ceaseless gra-
dation. . . . The last word never seemed to be able to
be uttered, for every end was a beginning, every last
result the first of a new opening.

Robert Musil, *The Man Without Qualities*

Nothing is harder to predict than the past.

A characteristic Czech joke
during the 1968 Prague Spring

It might be objected that even if my discussion of Appelfeld's novel
has succeeded in showing the judgmental callousness and historical
distortions to which backshadowing leads, I have done nothing to
challenge the notion that with a catastrophe as widely known and as
constitutive of the ethos of its century as the Shoah, backshadowing
is largely unavoidable. So deeply ingrained is our need to "make
sense" of even the most "senseless" calamities, and so powerful is
the urge to enfold even the harshest of experiences within a recog-
nizable pattern, that we have no choice but to draw upon the narrative conventions we have learned in other, less grievous cases or be
stunned into a permanent silence. And it is true that a reliance on
the most familiar and elementary building blocks of narrative emplotment often seems to increase in direct proportion to a story's
historical significance and repercussions. But the prevalence of a pattern is no proof of its necessity, and one of the major strengths of

Robert Musil's unfinished masterpiece, *The Man Without Qualities* (published in three volumes: 1930, 1933, 1943), is its principled resistance to exactly those conventions of foreshadowing and back-shadowing that writers like Appelfeld seem unable to do without.

The Man Without Qualities opens in August 1913, less than one year before the assassination of Franz Ferdinand, the heir presumptive to the Habsburg throne, at Sarajevo on June 28, 1914, which triggered, in rapid succession, Austria's deliberately unacceptable ultimatum to Serbia, a general European mobilization, and finally the outbreak of the First World War.[1] The pressures and twists of historical contingencies are central to the novel's unfolding, since Ulrich, its protagonist, reluctantly assumes the position of secretary of an elaborately ambitious but incoherent plan (the "Collateral Campaign") to celebrate the seventieth anniversary of the Emperor Franz Joseph's coronation, which would fall on December 2, 1918.[2] Conceived as a patriotic response to the prior German plan to honor their own emperor, Wilhelm II, on July 15, 1918, with a national festival celebrating his thirty years on the throne, the Austrian Collateral Campaign (*Parallelaktion*) is pathetically—as well as risibly—futile, since Franz Joseph himself was to die in 1916, and by the end of 1918 both the Austrian and the German empires would collapse and be replaced by republics. Musil's readers know from the outset that the political and social world the novel describes has very little time left before perishing in the conflagration of the war, so there is an unavoidable element of backshadowing in the irony with which the Collateral Campaign is described. But astonishingly, Musil does not use that knowledge as a basis for judging the actions and hopes of the characters in the book, nor is his ironic perspective on contemporary events determined by their historical outcome. The Collateral Campaign is *not* ludicrous because the ruler it planned to honor would be dead and his dynasty overthrown before the celebration's announced date, but because in its intellectual triviality and ideological blindness, the Campaign represented a ludicrous idea from the moment it was conceived. As Victoria Yablonsky, one of Musil's most perceptive American readers, has pointed out, the very existence of the *Parallelaktion* "rests on the [nonsensical] assumption that political unity *already exists* within the Empire, [the Campaign's] job [being] merely to express that unity.''[3]

In the salons and ministries of Vienna, the chance of a general European conflict is always kept in mind, but it is only one of a wide range of possibilities, and for the diplomats and soldiers most involved with questions of war and peace, avoiding such an outcome is precisely how they understand their life's work. *The Man Without Qualities* is full of intimations of the coming war, but it is just as resonant with suggestions that, finally, such an all-engulfing cataclysm can be prevented. The decisive point is how skillfully Musil allows the whole range of ideas and hopes held by his characters in 1913 to be heard clearly on their own terms. He regularly ironizes all of his characters' positions, but he does so only when their blindness and self-deception is manifest, and hence legitimately judgeable in the context of their own day, not when they fail to foresee the future. For example, General Stumm von Bordwehr, the military official who has attached himself to the Collateral Campaign, tells Count Leinsdorf, the Campaign's originator:

> I am convinced that almost everybody nowadays considers our era the best ordered one there has ever been. . . . The spirit of modern times actually lies in this great order and . . . it must have been some sort of muddle or other that brought the empires of Nineveh and Rome to a bad end. I believe most people . . . quietly go on the assumption that the past is past and gone as a punishment for something that wasn't quite in order. (321; 2:27)[4]

Characteristically, Musil's irony here is directed against, rather than dependent upon, backshadowing. The social tensions, ethnic rivalries, and irredentist violence that characterized the Empire in 1913 are quite sufficient to render absurd the General's blithe confidence in the existence of a uniformly contented citizenry enjoying a secure confidence in the stability of the social order. But sentiments like the ones just quoted are precisely what would have been uttered by an official like Stumm (whose name, quite unlike his personality, means "mute"), and the fact that in the utter chaos and disorder of the war these platitudes will soon be proved even more disastrously inaccurate does not make him any less sympathetic a figure or subject him to a greater degree of ridicule than the novel's more intellectually adroit characters. Analogously, when the emptily sophisticated senior bureaucrat of the Foreign Office, Tuzzi, says that "there's nothing so dangerous in diplomacy as amateurish talk about peace. Every time the craving for peace has risen to a given pitch and there was no more holding it, it's led straight into war," he is not foreshadowing the imminent disaster (1006; 2:406).[5] His comments are fully consonant with his already established professional opinions and interests and are intended to protect his "speciality," international diplomacy, from interference by amateurs like the members of the Collateral Campaign. That the war will soon break out may make this particular observation true, but it does nothing to validate most of Tuzzi's other judgments, and indeed it was the bungling and miscalculations of professionals of his stamp that helped turn a containable local crisis between Austria and Serbia into a continent-wide battleground. Both Tuzzi's accurate premonition and Stumm's erroneous one are independent of any external knowledge about the war, and are thus credible as contemporary utterances. Both men's pronouncements, that is, offer appropriate grounds for the narrator's irony in their own immediate context.

At its best, Musil's solution to the technical and epistemological problems raised by the narration of historical events whose outcome is already known is exemplary in its lucidity: because it is impossible for the reader to suspend his knowledge of the book's historical aftermath, the narrator will play upon that knowledge not in order to exploit it for the emotional intensities it might add to the story, but rather to undermine that readerly self-confidence by confronting it with a dense network of voices and ideas whose complexity and heterogeneity make the assumption of a superior, because subsequent, vantage point impossible. There are so many plausible scenarios for the future sketched out in *The Man Without Qualities,* so many different hopes and expectations voiced by characters in a position to make astute forecasts, that the entire novel swarms with projections of contradictory possibilities. It is as though *The Man Without Qualities* were all sideshadows, glimpses of diverse but equally credible futures, without any one of them being granted the aura of inevitability that is indispensable to foreshadowing; only because we know which of these projected futures came to pass are we tempted to privilege that one at the moment of its first articulation. But Musil specifically warns us against the intellectual triviality of such a judgment by satirizing the reader's inclination to endow a specific moment with greater portentousness strictly because of what ensued. It is *our* backshadowing that *The Man Without Qualities* regularly finds as absurd as the empty chatter of its fictional characters, and one of Musil's favorite satiric techniques, applicable equally to the discourse of figures in the book and to conventional readerly expectations, is to make explicit the link between foreshadowing and a naive trust in historical warning signs: "A new time had then just begun (for that is, after all, something that time is doing all the time). . . . These were stirring times, round about the end of 1913 and the beginning of 1914. But two years, or five years, earlier the times had also been stirring times" (20, 359; 1:51, 2:72).[6]

Just as Ulrich is deeply frustrated by the gulf between modern man's expert knowledge in the professional and scientific areas of life and the primitive assumptions with which he interprets the world as soon as he returns to his private life, so the novel as a whole seeks to undo, in the technical sense almost to deconstruct, the narrative conventions through which the reader imposes a linear, prescripted pattern on the motility of both historical events and individual psyches. Musil's irony works so effectively because he expects readers to approach a novel set on the eve of the Great War as though it would manifest all the familiar devices of interpretive foreshadowing, and thus they are already "set up" by their own assumptions to undergo the shock of realizing that they themselves, not just the book's characters, indulge in no-longer-credible patterns of thinking.[7] It is against such patterns and against the habits of mind that reinforce them that Musil directs some of his sharpest critiques. Life unfolds not only according to the "Principle of the Insufficient Cause," but along the lines of what modern mathematics calls a "random walk" rather than the predictable stages of any historical systematicity:

History, however, came into existence for the most part without any authors. It evolved not from a center, but from the periphery, from minor
causes. . . . The course of history was therefore not that of a billiard-ball,
which, once it had been hit, ran along a definite course; on the contrary,
it was like the passage of the clouds, like the way of a man sauntering
through the streets—diverted here by a shadow, there by a little crowd of
people, or by an unusual way one building jutted out and the next stood
back from the street—finally arriving at a place that he had neither known
of nor meant to reach. (360–361; 2:74–75)[8]

As we watch the Collateral Campaign set in motion forces that will
help create the necessary, but not sufficient, preconditions for World
War I, we see enacted a drama in which history unfolds without an
author or a script. Rather than one homogeneous authority planning
everything, competing centers of power (foreign affairs in the figure
of Tuzzi, the army with Stumm, international finance with Arnheim,
etc.) have separate and usually competing agendas. They form temporary and rapidly changing alliances, often with groups whose pur-
poses and beliefs are in many ways antithetical to their own. As in the
summer of 1914, it sometimes happens that the particular "local"
alliances that have coalesced for that moment become bound together into a single, long-term aim by the pressures of a larger event
that none of them had expected. But it is important to recall that no
one in charge expected or planned for a conflict of the magnitude
of World War I, nor did the various parties involved envisage any
permanent link to one another. For example, Musil shows us that
powerful voices in Austria's foreign service and army were preoccupied with building alliances designed to prevent the Empire from
becoming Prussia's junior partner. Yet against all the scheming of
some of Austria's most skilled political figures, that is precisely what
the Empire did become as soon as hostilities broke out. Through the
surprising tactical alliance of the Prussian businessman Arnheim and
the Austrian career officer Stumm, we witness how the fumblings of
the Collateral Campaign (which was, after all, conceived in a deliberately anti-Prussian spirit) helped to cement a German-Austrian affiliation, which was the one goal undesired by anyone involved in its
initial conception.

Because Musil's problem is so acute—how to tell a story that is set, like Appelfeld's, at the prelude to a universally known catastrophe, without allowing that catastrophe to dictate the mode of narration— he experiments with various solutions that are linked more through their family resemblance than by a set of fixed characteristics. One of the most ingenious of such strategies is elaborated in the following exchange between Ulrich and his cousin Diotima, the hostess in whose salon the Collateral Campaign regularly meets. They are talk- ing about General Stumm, and Diotima says, "I shudder from head to foot when I set eyes on him. He makes me think of death." Ulrich, who knows how peaceable and good-humored Stumm is, answers her, "A figure of Death unusually well disposed to life." But Diotima, as so often, has the last word and describes her feelings upon seeing the General: "But I am seized by panic when he comes up to me. . . . I'm overcome with an indescribable, incomprehensible, dreamlike sense of dread!" (466; 2:198).[9] By making the usually ridiculous Diotima, at whose vanity and pretentiousness the reader has often laughed, more prescient than Ulrich, the character with whose intelligence both the narrator and the reader tend to identify, Musil manages to incorporate the reader's inevitable awareness of the coming war with- out giving it any special authorial weight. If Ulrich were the one to regard Stumm as dangerous (i.e., to foresee in him one of the officers who would soon command men in operations of mass devastation) or, still more decisively, if the narrator were to do so, Diotima's in- tuition would be transformed into an instance of direct foreshadow- ing, or, more precisely, it would be Musil's backshadowing insertion of a knowledge of events unavailable to anyone in the book. But articulated as it is, the sense of dread at the incipient carnage is only an intuitive shudder by a character notorious for her capacity for self- delusion; the likelihood of war is thus incorporated into the novel but only, and thus entirely persuasively, as *one* of the possibilities in the air at the time.

Yet readers of *The Man Without Qualities* know that many of the novel's characters will die in the trenches, just as Appelfeld's readers know what awaits the Jews of Badenheim once they have boarded the trains. The lives of many of the Viennese in *The Man Without Qualities* are depicted as trivial and self-absorbed, and they are ironized as maliciously as are the assimilated Jews in Appelfeld's fiction. And since the futility of the hopes expressed in countless meetings of the Collateral Campaign is confirmed by the catastrophe of the Great War just as surely as the futility of the Jews' attempt to live in anti-Semitic Austria is made horribly evident by their murder in the camps, why does Musil's perspective seem so different from Appelfeld's judgmental fable?

One can begin to answer this question by stressing that the vacuity of the inner lives of most of Musil's characters, and the self-deception with which they defend their own interests, is exposed from within, partially by Ulrich's and the narrator's ironic commentaries and partially by Musil's technique of juxtaposing chapters on different characters as a means of indirect commentary on hidden—and usually unwelcome—similarities.[10] Musil's irony does not require a war to undermine the "true elite" (wahre Vornehmheit) of the Empire (what Graf Leinsdorf and Diotima smugly call the conjunction of Capital and Culture [Besitz und Bildung] in her salon).[11] Tonally, the war only risks disrupting the irony with pathos, and hence, except in some unpublished fragments, it is not directly narrated. Musil neither shows the war as inevitable nor uses it to confirm the misjudgments of his characters—indeed, some of them, like Arnheim, will come out of the disintegration of imperial Europe with their social position greatly improved. As Tuzzi observes, a Jewish capitalist like Arnheim (whom Musil based on Walter Rathenau [1867–1922], the German industrialist and Weimar foreign minister) could never rise to a cabinet position in a hereditary monarchy.[12] But although many of the characters in the novel would undoubtedly be killed in the war, the disintegration of their world is not due to their quotidian pettiness but rather to their inability to be quotidian enough. They regularly succumb to the appeal of the most rhetorically charged but contentless catchphrases of the moment, and the mobilization order that electrified Europe in 1914 would only be one more, although the most destructive, of such catchphrases. Hence, in *The Man Without Qualities,* unlike in *Badenheim 1939,* there is no need for the *frisson* of death imagery (the barbed wire, the restrictions on travel, the registration of inhabitants by the Health Ministry) to do the work of historical ironizing. Both Musil and Appelfeld rely on indirection and satire in order to avoid narrating the catastrophe as it is happening. But part of Musil's greater importance as a writer turns on the openness of his novel to conflicting voices and multiple, contradictory possibilities for the future: in other words, on his rejection of backshadowing in favor of sideshadowing. Even though he knows what their ultimate fate was likely to be, Musil, unlike Appelfeld, can imagine the history of his characters as not already predetermined. In both novelists' works, historical catastrophe acts as a final, brutal frame on the whole world of their books, but Musil does not see the frame as inevitable or all-explaining, nor does he rely on it to generate the story's emotional and thematic intensities.

Yet so accustomed are readers to the narrative orchestration which foreshadowing provides, that *The Man Without Qualities* is regularly misread as though it exemplified the very techniques it explicitly rejects. Most misreadings of Musil's novel proceed from the assumption that it is structured as a retrospective fable, not unlike *Badenheim 1939*. Thus, for example, Hannah Hickman sums up the terms in which the novel is typically interpreted:

> The whole work, but especially Book I, is to be seen as a portrait of a society moving inexorably towards war, like the passengers fast asleep in the train on course for collision. This inevitable outcome casts a shadow of irony over the entire narrative, as the various characters, each one a representative figure of the time, pursue their own concerns and seek their own salvation. Only Ulrich, the man without qualities, is clearsighted enough to perceive the sickness at the heart of civilisation, but his efforts to alert those in positions of power to the dangers ahead meet with almost total lack of comprehension.[13]

It is worth lingering for a moment on Hickman's phrasing, not merely because expressions like "casts a shadow . . . over the entire narrative" help confirm the appropriateness of my term backshadowing, but also because she invokes as self-evident the link between a belief in historical inevitability and a scorn for the realm of private, individual decisions that we already saw throughout *Badenheim 1939*.

In Hickman's view, to "pursue [one's] own concerns and seek [one's] own salvation" is inherently foolish or evil when an imminent crisis that people ought to be able to foresee is about to overwhelm everyone. But Musil, I believe, regarded the issue in diametrically opposite terms. The concern for his own moral, intellectual and spiritual "salvation" is virtually the only thing that deeply moves Ulrich. In fact, almost the last words of the published sections of *The Man Without Qualities* describe Ulrich as "fighting for his salvation" (1038; 3:442),[14] and the quest to understand himself and his situation in the world better is exactly what prompted him to take the "year's leave from his life" (47; 1:83) that is the novel's initial premise.[15] Indeed, many of the main characters in the novel speculate obsessively and continually about the great issues of the day and try with all their resources to direct the course of history. It is only "marginal" figures, men like Ulrich who lack the appropriate emotional "qualities" for public affairs, who renounce any attempt at historical efficacy and prefer to devote themselves to the care of their own states of mind. Similarly, the war was never seen as "inevitable" by Musil, for the very good reason that *nothing* in history can be so considered. The war is indisputably a pivotal turning point in world history, but its historical magnitude gives it no retrospective authority in *The Man Without Qualities.* Indeed, the most satiric parts of Musil's novel describe a world in stasis or in a self-perpetuating muddle, rather than on the verge of disintegration. The Habsburg Empire we actually are shown in Musil's pages could just as easily have lasted for many years more rather than collapse when it did (just as, for example, the Ottoman Empire survived for more than a century after observers were certain of its impending dissolution). The disintegration certainly happened, but occurrence, as *The Man Without Qualities* regularly instructs us, does not imply necessity.

Against any belief in historical necessity, Ulrich strives for what Musil calls a "conscious Utopianism" (16; 1:48).[16] His utopianism is grounded in "something that one can call a sense of possibility," and he is particularly careful to insist that "a possible experience or a possible truth is not merely the equivalent of a real experience or a real truth but lacking the value of being real" (16; 1:47–48).[17] The

sense of possibility contains a legitimacy of its own, both as an insti-
gation to action and as constitutive of human freedom. For Musil,
sideshadowing and a certain kind of utopian thinking are crucially
linked. But it is a utopianism radically different from the ideological
varieties that have rightly been criticized as dogmatically monolithic
and, in their historical consequences, have proved all too frequently
totalitarian.[18] Such critiques take as their target either fictional accounts of an *already achieved utopia* (e.g., Thomas More) or theoreti-
cal/political systems that claim *already to know* how to bring about a
utopia (Marxism, fascism, etc.). If the content of, or the path to utopia is already available in the present, and if one assumes that a single
model of utopia exists which is universally applicable, it is likely that
the utopian impulse will turn despotic, since only human selfishness
or ignorance, the effects of both of which can be curtailed by state
power, prevents the establishment of the ideal society.[19] But in Musil's
reformulation, utopian thinking is itself a form of sideshadowing, a
permanent awareness that *things might be different,* that the present
state of affairs and the future toward which people seem to be tending
are not the only possible ones. Such a utopianism can never be pre-
scriptive, because it does not presume to know the specific content
of the alternatives to the present. It knows only that they exist (here
the plural term is crucial because it is never a single utopia that is at
issue, but the existence of multiple, alternative presents and futures).
For Musil, the future ramifications of the present are potentially un-
limited, and this serves to guarantee human freedom in a way impossible with teleological readings of history or with a complacent
acceptance of whatever is, as legitimized by the sole fact of its concrete existence.[20]

Musil's typically ironic/serious way to underline this very point is
to deny the attribute of inevitability even to divine creation: "God
probably preferred to speak of His world in the subjunctive of poten-
tiality . . . for God makes the world and while doing so thinks that it
could just as easily be some other way" (19; 1:50).[21] This, in a sense,
is also the problem confronting the novelist: how to create a world
while still indicating that "it could just as easily be some other way."
As a result, and irrespective of those parts of the posthumous drafts

(the *Nachlaß*) in which Musil tries out having Ulrich go into combat, it is unlikely that the war could have been inserted successfully into the novel.[22] Only by setting his narrative before the outbreak of hostilities can Musil guarantee that neither his characters nor his narrator speak in the tones of predictive historical certainty. Because the war really did take place, there is too great a risk that its direct presence in the book would make it appear inevitable. Since Musil is so concerned to show that many things can be imagined as likely to happen, that numerous paths always exist, and that history is not driven by any rational principle or internal logic which would let the future be accurately predicted, he is also particularly careful not to allow the war to undermine the novel's fidelity to a sense of multifarious possibilities (*Möglichkeitssinn*). To include the war directly would risk giving it the privilege of not being just an *event* in the narrative, but rather its *meaning*, and this, precisely, is unacceptable to Musil.

Because of these deeply principled reasons, the scope of what was unacceptable put an enormous burden on Musil to create a structure that would suggest a *narratable* resolution to his theoretical/ethical requirements. That he in part failed to do so is clear not only from the incompleteness of the novel at the time of his death, but also from the nature of the last sections he actually published and the enormous mass of drafts and fragments he left behind. This is not the place to develop in detail my reading of these parts and their implications for understanding *The Man Without Qualities* as a whole, but because the question of foreshadowing and sideshadowing are so central to the issues involved, I want to outline briefly the terms of that reading.

Although a variety of reasons, including depression at the lack of an audience, an intermittent but long-standing "writer's block," intellectual exhaustion, and the financial uncertainties of an exile's life in Switzerland (where Musil and his Jewish wife, Martha, fled in 1938), have been advanced for Musil's inability to complete *The Man Without Qualities,* I think that once Musil rejected ending the novel with the melodramatic thunderclap of the outbreak of war (say, for example, the reading of a telegram announcing Franz Ferdinand's assassination at what would then obviously become the last meeting of the Collateral Campaign), the novel had to remain unfinished for strictly internal reasons. *The Man Without Qualities* is a novel that, for all its biting irony, struggles to achieve not a distance from the world, but an adequacy to the world's inherent complexity. A resolution in the text that remained entirely private (for example, the illuminations of Ulrich's and Agathe's "holy conversations") and had no correspondence in or influence upon the public world would be inherently unsatisfactory.[23] One way to crystallize what is at issue here is to understand that the "unfinishability" of *The Man Without Qualities* is closer to the open-endedness and potential interminability of Montaigne's work (whose individual essays, like the three published books of the *Essais* themselves, were revised many times during the life of the author to take into account new ideas, circumstances, or feelings) than to the Mallarméan project of the single, all-encompassing *Livre* that would absorb the entire, anarchic raw material of human life into its own depths and transform it into a sacred text, self-sufficient and autonomous. Montaigne's *Essais* and Musil's novel are "unfinishable" because the understanding of human existence expressed in their writings has no telos or single, unique meaning with whose realization their texts could end. Mallarmé's *Grand Oeuvre,* on the other hand, is in principle unrealizable because of the absolute split between word and world, between language as an autonomous object and the world of phenomenal (un)reality. For Musil, as for Montaigne, it is the inconclusiveness of life itself, both on the individual, biographical level and on the historical one, that makes the whole notion of closure so problematic.[24]

In the event, the only historically responsible climax was, as we have seen, exactly the one Musil could not draw upon directly without jeopardizing the main theoretical premises of much of his narrative. We can trace Musil's increasing preoccupation with the problem of how to end his novel, and one of the most revealing signs is the greatly increased, and often distressingly clumsy, introduction of foreshadowing as the novel continues and his confidence in being able to go on with and complete it becomes more and more uncertain. If, earlier in the *The Man Without Qualities,* interjections like "an appalling war with its millions of dead" (408; 2:129)[25] are surprising for their rarity, by the end of the last parts published during Musil's lifetime in 1933, their frequency and overemphatic nature steadily increase. Musil's anxiety about being able to complete his novel successfully is manifest not only in the backshadowing of historical events that he now allows to break his earlier restraint, but also in the foreshadowing of future occurrences in the purely private lives of his fictional characters. Thus, we now read sentences like "This was what Hagauer later termed Ulrich's being an accessory before the fact" (738; 3:95); "It was like a little rent in the vale of his life, through which indifferent nothingness peered. Here the basis was laid for much that happened later" (781; 3:145); or "Now this certainly did not mean that at this period Agathe already had the intention of killing herself" (855; 3:230).[26] But the most awkward examples of the strain in Musil's quest for an ending appropriate to the book's historical as well as personal spheres are audible whenever the narrator allows the shadow of the war to validate one of Ulrich's theories. Thus, in the final paragraphs to be published before Frisé's posthumous editions, Ulrich describes a general collapse of intellectual coherence and the corresponding increase in personal and social aggression: "The rubble of futile feelings, the rubble one age bequeaths to another has piled up as high as a mountain, without anything being done about it. So the War Ministry can sit back with its mind at rest, and wait for the next collective disaster." Had it been left in this form, Ulrich's pronouncement would be consonant with ideas both he and other characters have expressed throughout the novel and would represent only another, nonauthoritative prediction of what might happen. But then, in a single phrase, the narrator removes Ulrich's sentences from the realm of sideshadowing and gives them the retrospective inevitability of authorial backshadowing: "Ulrich was prophesying the fate of Europe, though he did not realize it" (1038; 3:442).[27] Ulrich may not realize that his speculations are, in fact, certainties, but both the narrator and the reader do, and it is fascinating to see how, whenever his self-confidence was at its most unsteady, Musil reverted to the narrative conventions he had earlier done so much to discredit.

But far more important than these instances of imaginative slackening is the fact that ultimately Musil chose *not* to rely on backsha-dowing to provide the coherent ending for which both he and his few remaining admirers longed. The war was permanently available as the great temptation to give *The Man Without Qualities* the kind of closure otherwise impossible to achieve, and the stubbornness of Musil's refusal to utilize it in this way, even at the cost of leaving his book incomplete, is the ultimate evidence of the centrality of sideshadowing in his thinking.

Here, the contrast with Marcel Proust is particularly illuminating. Proust, as we will shortly see, also recognized the intellectual and moral force of sideshadowing, but his commitment to the authority of a finished "great novel" in the classical tradition was even greater, hence his determination to end *À la recherche du temps perdu* with a movement of closure essential to a canonic masterpiece. In the event, Proust's longing for such an act of closure required a climactic set piece marked by a series of almost scandalously fortuitous coincidences (the famous rush of three separate episodes of involuntary memory at the *matinée* of the Princesse de Guermantes). But since Marcel went on to write the novel, triggered in part by these very accidents, they are now inscribed as decisive turning points in the narrative of a life that *needed* to be reinterpreted as a destiny in order for the story to be told at all. This conjunction of randomness and fate, although theoretically defensible, is too programmatic and didactic in its enactment to be entirely persuasive. Neither at the level of psychological motivation for Marcel's decision to begin writing, nor at the level of narrative plausibility for bringing the novel to a close, is such a series of almost Dickensian, "inevitable coincidences" adequate to the demands Proust places on them. What would have been required is an entirely new solution to the problem of ending a novel so that both contingency and necessity are equally registered: an epistemological perspective and a technical strategy that could manage to achieve a conclusion without seeming coerced or rigged. In order to dissipate a certain embarrassment at Proust's actual way of ending his book, the most theoretically adroit of his recent critics like Leo Bersani and Margaret E. Gray have tried to problematize his procedure, especially the relationship between Marcel and the novel's narrator: their readings suggest more ambiguity about the end than it probably possesses, in part, I think, because while that ending is all too unmistakably in accord with the formal requirements of a unified "classical" novel, it is dissonant with the richest insights and local unfoldings of the book itself, which depend on the multiplicity of perspectives and possibilities only sideshadowing makes narratable. The fundamental move of Bersani's suggestive new reading is to sever the link between the narrator of *À la recherche du temps perdu* and the aging Marcel, whom we watch resolving to go home and begin writing his life story after his shattering experiences at the Princesse de Guermantes' *matinée.* I disagree with Bersani's interpretation, and, for all its admitted awkwardness, accept the more conventional interpretation, which regards the narrator as the adult writer into whom Marcel painfully grows. I say so reluctantly, because if the identity of character and narrator were indeed separate, the novel would be even more expressive of a radical openness incompatible with foreshadowing than I think it actually is.[28] (In this context, it is worth asking whether a novel fully committed to sideshadowing ought to center on the life story of a single, clearly identifiable protagonist at all. Even Musil, for whom sideshadowing was a central intellectual/ ethical principle, had Ulrich's experiences dominate *The Man Without Qualities* still more than Marcel's dominate *À la recherche du temps perdu.* Perhaps only in works like Joyce's *Dubliners* (1914) or Dos Passos's *Manhattan Transfer* (1925) and *U.S.A.* trilogy (*The 42nd Parallel* [1930], *1919* [1932], and *The Big Money* [1936]), in which a whole city or historical era are the real "main characters," can sideshadowing be best enacted.)

Musil's inability to complete *The Man Without Qualities* should more properly be understood as his refusal to do so. In spite of the many temptations, evident in the later stages of the published sections and still more in the *Nachlaß,* he resisted artificially concluding the book's quest for a new kind of novelistic structure, a narrative order that did not rely on pre-established patterns. Instead, Musil left in fragmentary form the most serious response modern literature has yet provided to what he had recognized in an early essay as our need for "a type of intelligence . . . that would strive to discover and systematize the kind of knowledge that suggests new and daring directions to our emotions, even if these remain only pure plausibilities; an intelligence, that is, in which thinking would exist only to offer an intellectual framework to certain still undefined ways of being human.[29]

■ ■ ■

> Where you yourself were never quite yourself
> And did not want nor have to be,
> Desiring the exhilarations of changes:
>> Wallace Stevens,
>> "The Motive for Metaphor"

> What does not change / is the will to change
>> Charles Olson, "The Kingfishers"

Earlier in the book, I spoke about a certain readerly pleasure provided by works that flaunt their acceptance of mutually exclusive possibilities and make evident their unwillingness to enfold each narrative "accident" into the larger structure of the whole. In this countertradition, stories whose narratives at first seem structured like the biography of an actual human being can reveal themselves as utterly unconstrained by the most basic facts of human existence, including even the inevitability and irreversibility of death. In principle, a fictional character can have a limitless number of times to perform his life, can have *many,* not just one counterlife. In Yehuda Amichai's *Not of This Time, Not of This Place* (1963), for example, the main character, Joel, returns to his childhood home in Germany to find relics of his past and to plot acts of vengeance on the townspeople for their eager participation in the extermination of the town's Jews. But he is described as simultaneously staying in Jerusalem to throw himself into an affair with Patricia, an American gentile temporarily working in Israel as a doctor. Amichai is careful to keep the two logically incompatible plots linked through a complex, if occasionally forced parallelism of characters, events, phrases, and imagery in both sections, and the whole novel ends when Joel is accidentally killed while on reserve duty on Mount Scopus. Amichai, that is, welcomes the plurality of experiences, but permits only a unique and irreversible death in his fictional universe.

In *The Counterlife,* however, Philip Roth shows that a detailed description of a character's death in one chapter need not be binding for subsequent sections of the same book. Thus, Henry Zuckerman, whose death from a quintuple bypass operation is narrated in the first section, is also portrayed as having survived the surgery and gone to live with the disciples of a ferociously militant right-wing zealot in a West Bank Israeli settlement. Similarly, the novelist Nathan Zuckerman, Henry's brother, who tells us the story of Henry's death and then of his curious *aliyah,* is himself later described as having died of the very disease and operation he had attributed to Henry. Alternative and mutually exclusive destinies, love affairs, and moral obligations are tested in Roth's novel, with the result that the book as a whole is constituted as an exploration of the impulse to create a series of new existences for oneself and the cost of doing so.[30] In this sense, fiction is precisely what can reject fixity, and it offers the most unqualified enactment of our longing for fluid possibilities and limitless sideshadows. The desire to be free, at least in one's imagination, from the tyranny of one's own deepest convictions and the moral obligations they impose is part of the pleasure of novels that pluralize the confines of a strictly linear biographical narrative. But there are other factors involved as well, including an urge to crack the armature built up by even the most secure and respectable of one's accomplishments, in order to break free from the expectations scripted by previous successes. And because every success is always partial, always a compromise formation, sideshadowing can crystallize one's repugnance at all the half-measures and surrenders that lie behind the most glittering of triumphs. More generally, there is the longing to keep open imaginative options that any unique action or position, no matter how right, inevitably forecloses. It is this longing that the narrator of Louis Begley's *The Man Who Was Late* expresses when he thinks about his happily growing daughters. He does not regret any of their specific actions or choices; but he is saddened by the very act of feeling himself for the first time able to predict "what they would most probably be like as adults. There was nothing in what I saw that I could reprove, but the disappearance of other possibilities of development was in itself depressing."[31]

No doubt the pleasure yielded by the sudden lifting of conventional narrative and biographical constraints, celebrated in novels like those by Roth and Amichai, is dependent for its intensity on our long experience of the more restrictive models it contests. The refusal to satisfy an expectation of closure, as much as the appeal of tidy endings, only makes sense within the domain of narrative possibilities opened by figuration itself. But then, the question that Marcel Proust, more rigorously and relentlessly than any other writer, forces us to confront is why, at the level of our own self-understanding, are we so powerfully attracted to both foreshadowing and sideshadowing, even when we acknowledge them equally as only constructs of our own imagination? Why, in other words, does our pleasure in sideshadowing and our recognition of its liberating potential coexist with an equally powerful urge to accede to various deterministic master tropes of biographical and historical inevitability? In part, I think this is because of a hope that at a certain level biography will be revealed as destiny. The conviction that one's life can somehow be understood as having the inevitability of a classically arranged narrative can act as a barricade against the sometimes overwhelming nostalgia for paths *not* taken and regret for actions left undone. We want to convince ourselves that the life we ended up having was, from the outset, actually the only possible one. Because we are still such Platonists in our hierarchies, culturally trained to value only the necessary and essential, and because the "Principle of the Insufficient Cause" applies as much to our personal lives as it does to historical events, what one might call a "nostalgia for determinism" is triggered by the realization of the contingent and accidental character of much of our existence. Musil formulates this sense of frustration with typical irony: "After all, by the time they have reached the middle of their life's journey, few people remember how they have managed to arrive at themselves, at their amusements, their point of view, their wife, character, occupation and successes, but they cannot help feeling that not much is likely to change anymore. It might even be asserted that they have been cheated, for one can nowhere discover any sufficient reason for everything's having come about as it has. It might just as well have turned out differently"

(130–131; 1:177).[32] Yet so fundamental is our desire to see a necessary link between biography and fate that when the rupture between what were plausible expectations and the course of an actual life seems too enormous to incorporate into the conventional topos of a pragmatic "adjustment to a stern reality," we often think, in Cynthia Ozick's elegant formulation, that "his life as he was driven to conduct it was a distortion, not a destiny."[33]

At the same time, however, and in spite of the eagerness to believe that we actually had little choice in the choices we made, an overly forceful statement of pure determinism quickly provokes our resistance as well, just as in literature, too insistent a use of foreshadowing makes a text appear to lack verisimilitude and be clumsily manipulative in its structure. If everything that transpires is immediately marked as only a figure for some future event, the narrative may forfeit our identificatory sympathy with the characters' struggle to choose one action rather than another, and in so doing may eliminate an indispensable element on which our pleasure as readers depends. Hence the medieval, and particularly the Thomistic, insistence on the significance of the literal/historical, as well as the allegorical, moral, and anagogical senses of Scripture, and hence, too, Dante's effort to maintain the historical verisimilitude of his descriptions of contemporary Italy and his scrupulous care wherever possible to ground his immense allegorical structure in the circumstantial peculiarities of the historical moment. Without such care, an allegory quickly empties its "local" stories of any significance independent of its larger and all-encompassing meaning. Precisely such an emptying happened, as we have already seen, to the independent significance of the events narrated in the Hebrew Bible when they were allegorized as a cycle of prefigurations of the Gospel story by Church Fathers who neglected the most powerful principles of their own literary theorizing when it came to the Jewish sacred books. Paradoxically, Appelfeld treats the Jews of Badenheim much like the Christian exegetes treated the Jews of the Hebrew Bible, that is, as empty ciphers for an ahistorical moralizing allegory. And like all such allegories, Appelfeld's can never narrate historical events convincingly. Such writing is in its deepest nature atemporal, linking everything together into a permanently deferred but everywhere implied total vision. There can also never be any real sideshadowing in allegory. Historical events that unfold through time involve the succession of *nonnecessary* events and contain sideshadows at each moment of their unfolding; they are thus inherently in contradiction with the terms of an allegorical understanding/narration.

Like many seemingly intractable theoretical problems, the reliance upon the mutually exclusive notions of foreshadowing and sideshadowing in understanding our lives may appear self-contradictory when formulated in general terms, but recast more prosaically, it becomes far more amenable to understanding. One way to account for this double interpretative horizon is to see that what we commonly draw upon, without consciously articulating, is a kind of imprecise mediation between an entirely predetermined and a totally random explanation for our lives. This mediation seeks to persuade us that our lives took the paths they did on a kind of probability basis. That is, at every moment there were other courses possible for us, but each of these alternatives spoke to perhaps, ten, twenty, or even twenty-five percent of our needs and expectations at the time; the option we did take, however, hypothetically represented a greater percentage, perhaps on the order of thirty-five percent. The direction we followed was therefore not necessarily directed to satisfying the majority of our inclinations and ideas, but only to a sufficiently decisive plurality over any of the other potential routes we saw open at the time.

More subtly than any work of art I know, *À la recherche du temps perdu* probes the endlessly reconfigured relationships we establish between the different epochs of our lives, so that at times the characters' whole past seems like a preparation for and foreshadowing of their identity in the present, while at other moments, each episode exists almost inviolate in its own distinct sphere, with emotions and associations so rich in themselves as to make ludicrous the notion that they are preparatory to anything beyond themselves. Only in rereading do these early references assume any importance. Although in a sense akin to foreshadowing, they lack the inevitability and determinism of conventional foreshadowing, and often point to a whole range of sideshadowed possibilities. Proust creates *both* a special case of "only after the fact" foreshadowing (a foreshadowing that doesn't reveal itself as such until much later, and then only in a careful re-reading) and sideshadowing (he often traces alternative paths to the one taken), and he can do so because he believes simultaneously in destiny and chance, or, more accurately, he believes that terms like destiny and chance are neither historical nor biographical "facts," but tropes, constructs we create to make sense of our lives and give them the inner logic and form they would otherwise lack.

For example, early in *À la recherche du temps perdu,* Marcel mentions a quarrel with his parents "because I did not accompany my father to an official dinner where the Bontemps were to be present along with their niece, Albertine, a young girl still almost a child."[34] Since, in a few years, Albertine will become the overwhelming obsession of Marcel's life, there is something at once breathtakingly daring and entirely prosaic in the way Proust gives us a glimpse of a future that easily might have happened—an earlier meeting with Albertine and thus, perhaps, a different course to their love affair—which thereby would have changed utterly the course of the novel we are rereading. Even when Marcel's attraction to Albertine actually begins in *À l'ombre des jeunes filles en fleurs,* she is at first just one of the band of young girls, upon any of whom Marcel's desire might settle as easily as upon another, and among whom it hovers for many pages with pleasurably random motility. But once Marcel's imagination has isolated Albertine from amid her friends in the little band, his curiosity about her is remade, deliberately and remorselessly, into a devastating passion kept vivid with all the resources of Marcel's imaginative power.[35]

Marcel is both the reader and the novelist of his own life, creating, more than discovering, a plot that enables him to interpret his past as part of a coherent narrative. But that narrative is recognized from the outset as explicitly literary, and the emphasis of the novel is on the *work* required to create an adequately inclusive and unanticipatable interpretive structure. Moreover, the narrator's immense investment in the project of comprehending the impulses and needs that govern human conduct is regularly undermined, not so much because of the inherent psychological complexity motivating behavior, but rather because so many hypotheses could account equally for the same observable conduct. Proust draws upon all of the formal possibilities of sideshadowing to make clear the fundamental epistemological uncertainty into which the narrator, the protagonist, and the reader of the *Recherche* are all regularly plunged. From Marcel's central, lifelong obsessions with the "real nature" of Albertine's sexuality to the smallest details of social interaction, sideshadowing forces us to acknowledge the incoherence of our longing for a reliable, logically necessary explanation. Even so simple a question as why the Guermantes should treat their cousin, the Marquise de Gallardon, with aloof indifference proves unanswerable: "perhaps because she was boring, or because she was disagreeable, or because she was from an inferior branch of the family, or perhaps for no reason at all."[36] Yet not only may there be many motives for what happens, including some that do not occur to the narrator, but much of what we do and feel may take place "for no reason at all" (and here it is hard not to notice the similarity to Musil's "Principle of the Insufficient Cause"). This realization is itself finely balanced against the conviction that one can make sense, even if only retrospectively, of one's existence as the unfolding of a single, all-embracing narrative. The narrator's shifting perspective on the often contradictory paths that Marcel followed from Combray to the final *matinée* at the Princesse de Guermantes, the tense equilibrium between epistemological uncertainty and analytic assertiveness, and between an explanatory narrative based on pure accident and one based on ineluctable destiny is paradigmatic for the more general question of how we try to reconcile the competing attractions of foreshadowing and sideshadowing in our own lives, both as readers of texts and as interpreters of our own histories.

The retrospective/biographical model for interpretation is so appealing because, in James Young's phrase, it starts its narrative with a "full knowledge of the end, which inevitably contextualizes early experiences in terms of later ones."[37] In any narrative based on such a model, the first small detail is endowed with an importance it only acquired afterward and could not have had for the subject experiencing it for the first time. So Marcel's refusal to meet the Bontemps and their niece had no importance for the boy trying to cure himself of his love for Gilberte Swann, but reinterpreted from the vantage point of a man who remembers his love for Albertine as the most intense experience of his life, the refusal acquires a haunting irony. Marcel, who blames himself for so many failures, does not, at least, blame himself for this missed meeting, and it is difficult to imagine that any reader could fault him for an inadequate foreknowledge of his future passion.

Throughout these pages, my aim in having deliberately shifted the focus away from the Shoah to the story of an unrepresentative, socially privileged individual is precisely to see how the conventions of foreshadowing and backshadowing are also crucial in understanding how we make sense out of the vicissitudes of a unique, purely private existence.[38] I said at the outset that this is a book about narrative conventions and historical understanding, not about the Shoah as such, although it is the Shoah that provides the sternest test for my critique of backshadowing. No doubt, however, readers have been tempted to object that the situations Proust is narrating and the ones confronting the characters in *Badenheim 1939* are so radically dissimilar that it is simply incoherent to discuss them in analogous terms. At their most restrained and unemphatic, such objections might underscore that the pogroms and the political success of organized anti-Semitic parties in the late nineteenth and early twentieth centuries provided prior examples or a recurrent danger confronting European Jewry, whereas Marcel's missed meeting with Albertine was both completely accidental and unprecedented. And, of course, to compare the results of Marcel's refusal with the consequences of the Badenheim vacationers' self-deception reveals a disparity unbridgeable in its gravity. But Proust's novel, with its unparalleled richness of psychological/epistemological probing and the exactness of its account of how we continuously *construct* and *reconstruct*—novelistically—the meaning of our existence (our "destinies," in an older rhetoric), is especially pertinent because it engages so directly the problems of narrative and temporality central to our existence as beings who can only understand themselves through the stories they invent.

Paradoxically, when the domain in question is that of all-encompassing historical forces, a realm in which accurate foreknowledge would seem to be even less possible than in the restricted horizon of a single individual's self-knowledge, the demand for prescience actually increases rather than diminishes. We do not expect Marcel to know what he is missing by turning down the invitation from the Bontemps, but as we have seen in novels like Appelfeld's or histories like George Berkeley's, blame for their failure to foresee the future is assigned collectively to assimilated Austro-German Jewry in spite of the accompanying disclaimers that their fate was "unprecedented" and "unimaginable." One consequence that arises from a willingness to take seriously the Principle of the Insufficient Cause and the logic of sideshadowing in discussing the Shoah is to recognize that rethinking the history of European Jewry requires something other than assembling more facts about their lives and the manner of their extermination, invaluable as such research undoubtedly is. A compilation of data, no matter how complete, is not an argument, and an inventory of names, dates, and events, no matter how scrupulously assembled, is not an explanation. What is needed, I believe, is a change in the essential terms of the narrative models drawn upon in our accounts, so that on the one hand, the distortions inherent in foreshadowing are guarded against more carefully and, on the other, that the risks of an *in extremis veritas* interpretation of culture are questioned more self-consciously in our accounts. To think differently about the Shoah is to think differently and more prosaically about values in general, and although the Shoah must not itself be seen as the tragic instrument by which those prosaic values were made manifest, it brings into harsh focus the inadequacy of conventionally apocalyptic accounts.

6

(IN PLACE OF A) CONCLUSION
The Unmastered Future

> There is no total solution, but only a series of partic-
> ular ones.
> > Robert Musil, "On the Essay"

> Grammar does not possess a *final* tense.
> > Italo Svevo, "An Old Man's Confessions"

As we have seen, Yosef Yerushalmi is certain that the image of the
Shoah is "being shaped . . . in the novelist's crucible." Although, as
I argued earlier, there is little reason to assume that the novel is the
uniquely suitable medium for this subject to the exclusion of other
modes of representation, no doubt Yerushalmi has in mind the novel's rich legacy of formal experimentation in which the question of
how to narrate an extended historical sequence is given both theoretical and structural priority. The depiction of a collision between
vast and seemingly impersonal historical forces and a restricted set
of vividly particularized individuals is one of the triumphs of the
nineteenth-century novel, whose legacy and potential is far from
exhausted.

But questions of imaginative stance and narrative practice are ultimately much more significant than those of genre, and in order to
contest the apocalyptic and backshadowing rhetorics in which the
Shoah specifically, and Jewish history as a whole, have been figured
thus far, a prosaics of language and cultural interpretation is indispensable.[1] Prosaics, in this sense, would stress that in our culture it is
not the attractiveness of extreme risk or the darkest teachings of vi-

olence and domination that are repressed. Exactly these issues have long constituted an enormous, if not actually the major, portion of our intellectual conversation about history as well as about the human psyche. What *is* repressed, though, is the value of the quotidian, the counter-authenticity of the texture and rhythm of our daily routines and decisions, the myriad of minute and careful adjustments that we are ready to offer in the interest of a habitable social world. The celebration of the everyday, prosaic world, with its undramatic practices and values, has been conducted most obviously in the novel, but it occurs as well in poets as diverse as Horace, Auden, and Yehuda Amichai. This is obviously not the place to specify in more detail the contours of a principled defense of the quotidian, but it is not only considerations of space and immediate emphasis that make me resist the inclination to attempt such a description here. My understanding of how a coherent defense of prosaic ethics ought to proceed would be directly contradicted by the kinds of global and abstract formulations that are part of any systematic overview. The internal coherence and governing impulses of our habitual experiences and practices are too particular, too closely interwoven with changing contexts and circumstances to be caught up in and persuasively accounted for by universal categories.

The kind of ethics for which I am contending can better be enacted than formalized, and any adequate description must itself contain sufficient local depth and resonance to make vivid the lived world in which particular actions take place. In *The Blue Book*, Wittgenstein criticizes our "craving for generality" with its attendant "contemptuous attitude towards the particular case." He cautions us against trying to find a general concept behind all particular instances, saying that in logic, "the contempt for what seems the less general case . . . springs from the [erroneous] idea that it is incomplete."[2] In attempting to find a flexible and undogmatic basis for ethical distinctions, the need to ground one's thinking in a deep respect for particular cases is even greater than it is in formal logic, since it is only through close attention to a plurality of specific instances that the terms of a prosaic ethics can be articulated without becoming self-contradictory. Musil, who shared many of Wittgenstein's concerns, makes what is a

closely related distinction when he has Ulrich say, "There is no ethical program, but only an ethical condition."[3] This is why literature,
consisting, as it does, only of particular cases, is such a powerful re-
pository of the kinds of *exempla* that the search for an "ethical condition" requires. Rather than a series of moral imperatives, it is more
pertinent to point to novels like *The Man Without Qualities, Remembrance of Things Past,* or *Confessions of Zeno,* to uncategorizable works
like Montaigne's *Essays,* to prose meditations / memoirs like *Survival
in Auschwitz,* or indeed to many of the other texts mentioned in the
course of this book, for a vital engagement with ethical questions. It
is notoriously difficult to articulate these concerns without falling into
a kind of restrictive and unself-questioning Arnoldian high moral-
ism.[4] But one important distinction is that contrary to much of what
is considered "advanced" thinking in contemporary criticism, I believe that the role of theory should only be to illuminate practice,
never to dictate it. For example, it is precisely the scrupulousness of
Primo Levi's care for the specifics of individual experience and his
reluctance, even when confronting the enormity of Auschwitz's daily
horrors, to offer moralizing generalizations about human nature or
history, that help make his writings about the Shoah so luminous. But
we can also hear echoes of an analogous care in other texts, including, at the level of historico-philosophical argument, Amos Funkenstein's few but compelling pages on the Shoah.[5] Funkenstein provides
one of the rare examples of steadfastly prosaic reflections on the
Shoah, arguing that no matter what the situation, "human life and
the incommensurable value of each individual" must be regarded as
absolute. He denies the significance of the schism "between authentic and inauthentic existences" fundamental to thinkers like Heideg-
ger, and insists that "from an ethical point of view every life is authentic, a value in and of itself, not interchangeable with any other
human life, a mode *sui generis.*" To respect what Funkenstein calls
"the integrity and worthiness of each concrete individual life, however lived" is fundamental to prosaics, as is the rejection of the belief
that it is a "crisis—say, war and destruction, . . . [which] 'calls' man
to his true self."[6]

     Yet, as we have seen, the division between authentic and inauthentic lives is as basic to *Badenheim 1939* or to Zionist attacks on the false consciousness of assimilated Jews as it is to Heideggerian-inspired existentialism, and the faith that moments of crisis and extreme stress will reveal the truth about human nature is almost constitutive of all writing—whether historical or literary—about the Nazi genocide. However, what literature is particularly able to do is either reinforce or contest the patterns of thinking that nourish such a coercive understanding of our existence. Invested with the right proportion of passion and lucidity, a work of fiction can combine an absolute respect for the historical facts with a sense of the need for new narrative models within which to understand and articulate those facts. Moreover, the novel, in Walter Benjamin's understanding, is marked by a meticulous attention to the "incommensurability" and "perplexity" of individual existence,[7] and the need to keep in mind that incommensurability is all the greater, just as its concrete realization is all the more difficult, when the historical fate of a large majority of the narrative's characters is a bureaucratically administered mass murder.

Nineteenth- and twentieth-century Russian literature, to invoke a powerful supporting model, always kept alive a sense of the moral accountability of the act of writing, and in both prose and verse it managed to create a heritage of permanently renewed "tales of the tribe" in which the trials and "perplexity" of unmistakably individualized figures was immediately understood as emblematic of the nation as a whole. From Dostoevsky's *Notes from the House of the Dead,* to Akhmatova's cycle of poems "Requiem," to Solzhenitsyn's *One Day in the Life of Ivan Denisovich* and *The Gulag Archipelago,* Russian authors and their audience never lost the certainty that prose fiction and poetry were equally indispensable for interpreting the horrors of their history. For twentieth-century Jewish history, and especially for the Shoah, narrative histories, survivor memoirs, films, and poetry can all participate along with the novel in telling the communal tale, and each will find itself pressed by the demands of the subject matter to extend the responsiveness and responsibilities of its own idiom. In this way, it is possible to imagine a series of texts (certainly no single one could suffice) that would begin the task of shaping our view of the Shoah in new ways. In fact, of course, the project of trying to write about the Shoah began in the ghettos of Eastern Europe simultaneously with the Nazi genocide itself. But particularly after the war, ever since the full horror of the death camps has become part of our general knowledge, the increasing availability of so many kinds of narratives, expressed in every medium, testifies to a common recognition of how significant the attempt at giving expression to the Shoah is for our culture. It is also an important reason why I am less distressed than are many others at the inevitable vulgarizations that have accompanied such an outpouring of narratives. It is true that these debased versions can displace and preempt more morally and intellectually responsible accounts, but since learning how to tell the story is in itself almost as significant as communicating a series of historical facts, even the more appalling lapses into exploitation and facile mythologization can have the salutary effect of discrediting certain tones and devices, thereby forcing more scrupulous artists to rethink their own premises.

I am not concerned in this discussion to question the literary strength of works written from perspectives that rely on historical or theological certainties, when those perspectives still corresponded to the ways society understood and made sense of human existence. The problem in the modern world, as Robert Musil so clearly understood, is that at the level of epistemology, historiography, and logic we have long ceased believing in the authority of precisely those explanatory principles that we nonetheless continue to rely upon to structure our narratives of historical causality and personal development. Hence the sense of either strain and unease, or of naïveté and reductiveness that marks so many historical and psychological narratives. The urge to find a new way to tell our stories is not due to any faddish longing after novelty, or to a careless dismissal of the masterpieces of the past, but rather to an urgent need to find a narrative strategy that adequately expresses the full range of intellectual premises of our own epoch as persuasively as earlier stories corresponded to, or self-consciously challenged the basic convictions and assumptions of their times. The task for us as both storydwellers and storytellers,[8] that is, as individuals who learn to understand ourselves and our world

through the stories we tell and are told, is how to construct the meanings we require in our personal and collective narratives without hy-
postatizing those narratives as absolute and inevitable.

Thus far, to return to the hardest of test cases, it seems to me that
it is in poetry that the Shoah has been given its most searching artic-
ulations. The writing of Paul Celan (1920–70) has shown that it is
possible to write about the experience of the camps and be compelled
by one's own native linguistic inheritance and genius to do so in the
very language of the murderers—indeed, to make out of that terrible
necessity the fulcrum of what remains the one indispensable body of
verse written by a Western European during the past thirty years. But
if Celan finally created, and it is scarcely necessary to insist at how
terrible a price, a language commensurate with the bitterest destiny
of his people, there are other contemporary writers who have found
a voice more firmly pitched in the prosaic register of daily experience
with which they can express both a wider sweep of Jewish history and
a more inclusive ethic for the future of the tribe. Contrary to expectations that link prosaics too restrictively with the novel, several of
these writers of an anti-apocalyptic middle voice are poets. I want
again to invoke one of these poets, Yehuda Amichai, not only because
he seems to me the strongest writer of his generation in Israel as well
as one of the preeminent poets active in any tongue today, but also,
and more specifically, because his work so strenuously resists the twin
urges toward an apocalyptic and an accusatory backshadowing rhetoric.

No doubt, there are many other possible ways to end this book.
This is just one of them. But I have chosen to close with the exemplary
figure of Amichai, rather than, for example, with Paul Celan's more
intense but also more lonely and austere vision, because at his best,
Amichai epitomizes an intelligence, sensibility, and tonal range that
is forging new ways to make Jewish history narratable without sub-
ordinating it to any of the more readily available rhetorical and narrative models. It is not of incidental importance that Amichai emigrated to Israel from Germany in 1936 as a twelve-year-old adolescent.
He was old enough, in other words, to have witnessed first-hand the
growing savagery of his native country, but unlike Celan, he did not

have to endure the ultimate horrors which that savagery inflicted on the Jews. Amichai served with the Jewish Brigade in the Second World War; he fought as an infantryman in the Israeli War of Independence and thus saw enough combat and bloodshed to be thoroughly repelled by the thematics of a redemptive violence as the catalyst of higher truths.

What Amichai has achieved in a number of poems is to create an immediately visualizable image of sideshadowing, a way to make us actually turn our gaze away from the central, apocalyptic expectations of a uniquely redemptive history, toward the prosaics of a history figured in terms of its most quotidian exigencies. In one of these poems, "Tourists," Amichai describes the usual Jewish visitors to Jerusalem "sitting around at the Holocaust Memorial, putting on a serious face / at the Wailing Wall, / . . . / They get themselves photographed with the important dead / at Rachel's Tomb and Herzl's Tomb, and up on Ammunition Hill." At this point, one begins to fear that the rest of the poem will proceed by a series of facile antitheses between the insensitive, even exploitative, tourists—*Galut* Jews eager to appropriate the daring of the Zionist heroes without having had to take the risks Israelis faced building and defending their nation—and the passionate Jerusalemite narrator whose knowledge of what these shrines really mean is intended to put the travelers' reactions to shame. Such a poem would actually be just a thinly transformed version, expressed through the too conveniently at-hand example of Jewish history, of the conventional topos of a sensitive poet confronting the ignorant philistines—in other words, merely a modulation of the most formulaic of romantic commonplaces into the terms of Zionist typology. But then, as though the earlier lines had been intended precisely as a warning of how easily his motifs could miscarry and be misused, Amichai ends "Tourists" with the strictest, but nonpunitive, undermining of the facile antitheses it has evoked. And if one thinks back to the discussion of the narratives of Austro-German Jewry with which I began, it will be clear why I am also willing to stop here, letting the poet's words serve as the best evidence that a new relationship to Jewish history is possible, a poetics in which both the painful and the richly enduring legacy of that history, as well as the framework for a different future, begin to find their rightful measures:

> Once I was sitting on the steps near the gate at David's Citadel and I put down my two heavy baskets beside me. A group of tourists stood there around their guide, and I became their point of reference. "You see that man over there with the baskets? A little to the right of his head there's an arch from the Roman period. A little to the right of his head." "But he's moving, he's moving!" I said to myself: Redemption will come only when they are told, "Do you see that arch over there from the Roman period? It doesn't matter, but near it, a little to the left and then down a bit, there's a man who has just bought fruit and vegetables for his family."[9]

Notes

1. AGAINST FORESHADOWING

1. As I explain in the Acknowledgments, the term *sideshadowing* was originally coined by Gary Saul Morson and is central to his book, *Narrative and Freedom: The Shadows of Time* (New Haven: Yale University Press, 1994). I then coined the corollary concept of *backshadowing,* and at one time Morson and I thought of publishing our work together as a single, two-part study. For all their differences in focus and areas of concern, *Foregone Conclusions* and *Narrative and Freedom* are linked in fruitful ways and can be read as two voices in what has become a newly emerging critical counter-tradition that unites ethics and exegesis from an anti-utopian and anti-systematic perspective.

2. In 1 Corinthians 10:6, Paul writes of the Jews in the desert, "Haec autem in figura facta sunt nostri" (These events happened as symbols to warn us). The original Greek verses, in which the Jews are called *typoi hemon* (figures of ourselves), make the scope of the appropriation still clearer. Amos Funkenstein points out that when "Christian polemics spoke of the 'blindness' of the Jews (*caecitas Iudaeorum*)," it was precisely because Jews were "unable to detect in the old dispensation the foreshadowing of the new." Funkenstein, "Franz Rosenzweig and the End of German-Jewish Philosophy," in his *Perceptions of Jewish History* (Berkeley and Los Angeles: University of California Press, 1993), 300. For a discussion of the history and literary force of Christian figural typology, see Erich Auerbach, "Figura," in his *Scenes from the Drama of European Literature* (Minneapolis: University of Minnesota Press, 1984), 11–76. On the way the Hebrew Scriptures were consistently transformed within the Christian hermeneutical tradition, see Rowan A. Greer, "The Christian Bible and Its Interpretation," in James L. Kugel and Rowan A. Greer, eds., *Early Biblical Interpretation* (Philadelphia: Westminster Press, 1986), 107–208.

3. Jonathan Boyarin, *Storm from Paradise: The Politics of Jewish Memory* (Minneapolis: University of Minnesota Press, 1992), xv. My argument here is not intended to deny that Judaism, too, has been powerfully shaped by a providential reading of history, one in which foreshadowing is a central nar-

rative device. The concept of history being controlled by God for the direct reward or punishment of the Jewish people, from the parting of the Red Sea to the military victories of the Six Day War, is fundamental to many religious Jews. However, Jewish theology is neither supersessionist nor progressivist in the sense I have described: unlike Christianity, that is, Jewish thinkers did not interpret the texts of another religion as earlier, incomplete prefigurations of their own narratives, and hence they had no reason to conceive of time as a progression from partial blindness to full vision.

4. Robert Musil, *Der Mann ohne Eigenschaften,* ed. Adolf Frisé (Reinbek bei Hamburg: Rowohlt, 1978), 134: "Das Prinzip des unzureichenden Grundes! . . . Sie . . . wissen was man unter dem Prinzip des zureichenden Grundes versteht. Nur bei sich selbst macht der Mensch davon eine Ausnahme; in unserem wirklichen, ich meine damit unserem persönlichen Leben und in unserem öffentlich-geschichtlichen geschieht immer das, was eigentlich keinen rechten Grund hat." All references are to this edition and are acknowledged in the body of the text. The English translation quoted is by Eithne Wilkins and Ernst Kaiser, *The Man Without Qualities,* 3 vols. (London: Secker and Warburg, 1966), 1:181. I have modified Wilkins and Kaiser's formulations when the German seemed to require such a change. Source citations for *Der Mann ohne Eigenschaften* indicate the page number in the German text, followed by the volume and page number in the Wilkins and Kaiser translation. The German text is found in the notes.

5. Philip Roth, *The Counterlife* (Franklin Center, Pa.: Franklin Library, 1986). The whole of Roth's two-page preface to the Franklin Library Edition of his novel is interesting as an example of the kinds of themes he was pondering during the book's composition. Paradoxically, one of the things that makes his list intriguing is its very dullness and conventionality as literary formulae. Here, if anywhere, the enormity of the gulf between the lived richness of a fictive imagination and the relative barrenness of its theoretical promptings is evident.

6. Roberto Calasso, *The Marriage of Cadmus and Harmony,* trans. Tim Parks (New York: Knopf, 1993), 22. Often, Calasso's description of mythical narration sounds like a recapitulation of Philip Roth's note to *The Counterlife:* "Stories never live alone: they are the branches of a family that we have to trace back, and forward. . . . Everything that happens, happens this way, or that way, or this other way." (10, 147)

7. Jasper Griffin, "Alive in Myth," *New York Review of Books,* vol. 40, no. 8 (April 22, 1993): 25–26.

8. Hermann Broch, *Die Schlafwandler: Eine Romantrilogie* (Frankfurt:

Suhrkamp, 1978). See, for example, the description of Hanna Wendling in part 3, chapter 38, or of Ludwig Gödicke in part 3, chapter 56.

9. For a lucid summary of the changing interpretation of Freudian over-determination, see J. Laplanche and J.-B. Pontalis, *The Language of Psycho-Analysis*, trans. D. Nicholson-Smith (New York: W. W. Norton, 1973), 292–93.

10. On the concept of "various chains of meaning" intersecting at the "nodal point" of a symptom, see Laplanche and Pontalis, *Language of Psycho-Analysis*, 293.

11. Just as each life can have a multitude of counterlives, so each history is accompanied by numerous potential counterhistories, not all of which will ever be narrated. Amos Funkenstein has defined perhaps the most common kind of counterhistory as a "specific genre of history written since antiquity [whose] function is polemical. Their method consists of systematic exploitation of the adversary's most trusted sources against their grain. . . . Their aim is the distortion of the adversary's self-image, of his identity, through the deconstruction of his memory." Amos Funkenstein, "History, Counter-history, and Narrative," in Saul Friedlander, ed., *Probing the Limits of Representation: Nazism and the "Final Solution"* (Cambridge: Harvard University Press, 1992), 69; reprinted in Funkenstein, *Perceptions of Jewish History*, 36). As examples of explicitly polemical counterhistories, Funkenstein gives "Manetho's hostile account of Jewish history, based largely on an inverted reading of Biblical passages," Augustine's *De Civitate Dei* ("A veritable counter-history of Rome"), the seventh-century Jewish *Sefer Toldot Yeshu* ("Narrative of the History of Jesus"), in which Jesus is described as a corrupt magician intent on "seducing the unlearned multitude," and Protestant historiography (intent upon "the construction of a counterhistory of the Church"). Funkenstein, "History, Counterhistory, and Narrative," in Friedlander, *Probing the Limits of Representation*, 71–73; reprinted in Funkenstein, *Perceptions of Jewish History*, 39–41.

2. BACKSHADOWING AND APOCALYPTIC HISTORY

1. This description is found in Gary Saul Morson, "Genre and Hero/ *Fathers and Sons:* Inter-generic Dialogues, Generic Refugees, and the Hidden Prosaic," *Stanford Slavic Studies*, vol.4, no.1 (1991): 336–81. The phrase about seeing reality with "the eyes of the genre" is from P. N. Medvedev and M. M. Bakhtin, *The Formal Method in Literary Scholarship*, trans. A. J. Wehrle (Baltimore: Johns Hopkins University Press, 1978), 134.

2. *Holocaust* is derived from the Greek *holokauston* used in the Septuagint in the sense of "totally consumed by fire." In the Septuagint it refers specifically to sacrifice by fire, assonant with the Hebrew term for sacrificial offering, *olah*, which, as Berel Lang explains, "designates the type of ritual sacrifice that was to be completely burnt (as in Leviticus 1:3ff.). The English usage of 'holocaust' in the sixteenth and seventeenth centuries elaborated this literal sense of a religious burnt offering; later, the term began to appear as a metaphor for sacrifice more generally. In the seventeenth and eighteenth centuries, the term characteristically appears in reference to the complete destruction of an object or place or group, most often by fire, but also by other (mainly natural) causes. . . . Both the Hebrew designation *shoah* ('wasteland' or 'destruction,' as in *Isaiah* 10:3 and *Proverbs* 3:25) and the Yiddish variation of the Hebrew *churban* ('destruction')—the latter traditionally applied to the destruction of the Temples and then reapplied metonymically to other destructions—are more accurately descriptive than 'Holocaust,' because they imply a breach or turning point in history (*and because they reject the connotation of 'sacrifice'*)." Lang, *Act and Idea in the Nazi Genocide* (Chicago: University of Chicago Press, 1990), xxi. James Young points out that "holocaust in the present sense didn't become the preferred term until between 1957–59," and gives the history of some of the other ways the language tried to define (and thereby implicitly interpret) the unprecedented Nazi attempt to exterminate all Jews: "the Hebrew term *churban* ['destruction'] suggested itself immediately . . . [but] its Yiddish echo (*churbn*) and explicitly religious association made *churban* less appealing to Labor Zionists in Palestine. . . . As a result the term *sho'ah* was adopted . . . marking the event as part of Jewish history but avoiding comparisons with specific precedents." Young, *Writing and Rewriting the Holocaust: Narrative Consequences of Interpretation* (Bloomington: Indiana University Press, 1988), 85–86. But even *sho'ah*, although in many ways preferable to other designations, is not without unwelcome implications of its own. As Chana Kronfeld pointed out to me, the modern Hebrew usage of *sho'ah*, when it does not refer specifically to the Nazi genocide (in which case it is almost invariably preceded by the definite article, *ha-sho'ah*), is used for natural disasters like earthquakes or floods (*sho'ah teva* means "natural catastrophe"), that is, it designates events for which no human agent can be held responsible and which, therefore, are not subject to moral judgment. See also Uriel Tal, "Excursus on the Term *Shoah*," in *Shoah: A Review of Holocaust Studies and Commemorations*, vol. 1, no. 4 (1979): 10–11.

3. Irving Howe, "Writing and the Holocaust," in Berel Lang, ed., *Writing and the Holocaust* (New York: Holmes and Meier, 1988), 190.

4. Yael Feldman has studied "the extent to which Israeli culture … attempted to assimilate the experience of the Shoah to its overall Zionist perspective." During her childhood in Israel, when the Shoah was discussed, "centerstage was occupied (and quite literally so) by school plays about the Warsaw uprising or the heroic mission of Hanna Senesh. For us *Yom hashoah vehagvurah* (Day of Holocaust and Heroism) was not 'Martyr's Day,' as my *current* Israeli calendar translates it, but rather a celebration of resistance and national pride, a prolegomena to the Israeli Day of Independence." Yael S. Feldman, "Whose Story Is It Anyway: Ideology and Psychology in the Representation of the Shoah in Israeli Literature," in Saul Friedlander, ed., *Probing the Limits of Representation: Nazism and the "Final Solution"* (Cambridge: Harvard University Press, 1992), 223. See also Saul Friedlander, "Die Shoah als Element in der Konstruktion israelischer Erinnerung," *Babylon* 2 (1987): 10–22. For a fascinating comparative study of the ways the Shoah has been taught in schools in Germany, Israel, and the United States, see Randolph L. Braham, ed., *The Treatment of the Holocaust in Textbooks* (New York: Social Science Monographs and Institute for Holocaust Studies, 1987).

5. Primo Levi's *Se questo è un uomo*, misleadingly renamed in English as *Survival in Auschwitz*, rather than as "If This Is a Man," trans. Stuart Woolf (New York: Macmillan, 1961), 82.

6. I say uncannily delayed because one of the more surprising aspects of Hebrew literature is that, in Alan Mintz's description, "between World War II and the Eichmann trial in the early sixties there are no significant works of Hebrew literature which directly engage the Holocaust, with the major exception of [the poet] Uri Zvi Greenberg." Mintz, *Hurban: Responses to Catastrophe in Hebrew Literature* (New York: Columbia University Press, 1984), 158. It is true, of course, as several readers including Robert Alter and Chana Kronfeld have commented, that poets like Nathan Alterman, Amir Gilboa, and Hayim Gouri did write significant poems about the Shoah before the Eichmann trial, which began in April 1961. But Mintz's description of Israeli prose fiction is fundamentally accurate and characterizes one of its most problematic aspects. I explore some of the context and consequences of this delayed response in the section on Aharon Appelfeld.

7. Young, *Writing and Rewriting the Holocaust*, 134.

8. My argument here is in no way metaphorical. On the contrary, similar demographic calculations were among the ways in which it first became known how many millions of Russians had been killed during Stalin's years

in power. See Robert Conquest, *The Nation Killers: The Soviet Deportation of Nationalities* (New York: Macmillan, 1970); *The Harvest of Sorrow: Soviet Collectivization and the Terror-Famine* (New York: Oxford University Press, 1986); and *The Great Terror: A Reassessment* (New York: Oxford University Press, 1990). Estimating what the population would have been without the mass killings requires "counting" the descendants not born to the murdered, and this is true for all historical catastrophes, not merely for the Nazi or Stalinist brutalities. Thus, for example, Alan Bullock estimates that "fifteen million men, women, and children . . . perished in the [Russian] civil war itself and the subsequent famine—sixteen or seventeen million in all for the years 1914 to 1922, if one adds those soldiers and civilians killed during the First World War. Russia's population in 1923 was about thirty million less than would have been expected from projections of the earlier figures." Bullock, *Hitler and Stalin: Parallel Lives* (New York: Knopf, 1992), 103.

9. Lang, *Act and Idea in the Nazi Genocide*, 214.

10. Lawrence L. Langer, *Holocaust Testimonies: The Ruins of Memory* (New Haven: Yale University Press, 1991), 205.

11. Michael Ignatieff, "The Rise and Fall of Vienna's Jews," *New York Review of Books*, vol. 36, no. 11 (June 29, 1989): 21.

12. Ibid., 22–24. Here it might be helpful to think of the distinction, long current in the social sciences, between logical and probabilistic conceptions of cause and effect. Such a distinction helps crystallize the idea that, to the people involved in making decisions, future developments which plausibly appear to be the least probable can, in fact, occur, while the most probable possibilities never actually come to pass. Clearly, a probabilistic understanding of causality entails more flexible attributions of responsibility for the results of specific actions than does a historically deterministic or strictly logical model. (I owe the suggestion to include these considerations to one of the readers of my manuscript for the University of California Press.)

13. Ernst Pawel, *The Nightmare of Reason: A Life of Franz Kafka* (New York: Farrar, Strauss and Giroux, 1984), 25.

14. Ibid., 60.

15. Ibid., 376.

16. For a different, although related perspective on the link between Nazi imagery and kitsch, see Saul Friedlander, *Reflections of Nazism: An Essay on Kitsch and Death*, trans. Thomas Weyr (New York: Harper and Row, 1984).

17. See, for example, Ruth Wisse's review, "The Jew from Prague," *Commentary*, vol. 78, no. 5 (November 1984): 62–64. Theodore Ziolkowski even calls the book "likely to be the definitive biography for some time to come

in *any* language"; *World Literature Today,* Winter 1985, p. 86. John Updike, not surprisingly, is the least persuaded of Pawel's numerous reviewers. He maliciously compares Pawel's literary tone to the famous " 'booming parade-ground voice' of that much-maligned father Hermann Kafka." More important, Updike records his discomfort with the way the biographer's "insistent references to the coming Holocaust shadow his narrative of Kafka's life" until "there is a danger of making Hitler the hidden hero of that story and the Holocaust its culminating event." John Updike, "The Process and the Lock," *New Yorker,* June 18, 1984, pp. 108, 111.

18. George S. Berkeley, *Vienna and Its Jews: The Tragedy of Success* (Cambridge, Mass.: Madison Books / Abt Books, 1989), 87.

19. Arthur C. Danto, *Analytical Philosophy of History* (Cambridge: Cambridge University Press, 1965), 12.

20. Mintz, *Hurban,* 226.

21. Pawel, *Nightmare of Reason,* 328.

22. George Steiner, *Language and Silence* (New York: Atheneum, 1966), 50.

23. Frederick Karl, *Franz Kafka: Representative Man* (New York: Ticknor and Fields, 1991). The general tone and level of moral scrupulousness of Karl's book can be gauged by the dedication: "To the 6 million, Europeans murdered by Europeans." Leaving aside the curious and confused decision to describe the murdered simply as "Europeans," a polemical move that makes little sense when one considers that the total number of Europeans who died in World War II enormously exceeded the six million Jews butchered by the Nazis, there is the more serious question of how the biography of even the most brilliant modern Jewish writer could possibly serve as a fitting memorial to the victims of the Shoah. The disproportion between the offering and what is being commemorated is so great that it approaches the grotesque.

24. Ibid., 471, 494.

25. Ibid., 725n.

26. A useful contrast here is offered by the more modest and historically nuanced comment by William McCagg in *A History of Habsburg Jews, 1670–1918* (Bloomington: Indiana University Press, 1989), 179–80: "Turn-of-the century Bohemian Jewry is the reputed source of Kafka's expressions of human agony. Kafka's apparent slavery to words—the agony with which slowly, slowly he followed words first into aphoristic expression, later into stories and never-completed novels; his inability to decide; his failure to finish; his extraordinary sensitivity to double meanings—all this can be associated with

the 'in-betweenness' of the Jewish world in which he grew up. One may doubt certain aspects of some of the more deterministic assessments of Kafka: it is not certain, for example, that from the start his creative career was assertively Jewish—he seems rather to have discovered his identity when he was well along. Further, Bohemian Jewry's malady was perhaps less 'in-betweenness' than pronounced 'slipping and sliding' of the late nineteenth century.''

27. The discussions between Benjamin and Scholem constitute the most impassioned and lucid commentary on Kafka that I know. In addition to numerous passages throughout Scholem's various memoirs, especially *From Berlin to Jerusalem: Memoirs of My Youth,* trans. Harry Zohn (New York: Schocken, 1980) and *Walter Benjamin: The Story of a Friendship* (trans. Harry Zohn (New York: Schocken, 1981), the key text of their discussion is *The Correspondence of Walter Benjamin and Gershom Scholem, 1932–1940,* trans. Gary Smith and Andre Lefevere (New York: Schocken, 1989). The best critical study of the crucial imaginative triangulation of Kafka, Benjamin, and Scholem is Robert Alter's *Necessary Angels: Tradition and Modernity in Kafka, Benjamin, and Scholem* (Cambridge: Harvard University Press, 1991).

28. The lines from *Mein Kampf* are quoted in Lucy S. Dawidowicz, ed., *A Holocaust Reader* (New York: Behrman House, 1976). As Alan Bullock points out, referring to both Stalin's and Hitler's increasingly tyrannical and murderous regimes, ''It is not only the appetite for power that grows with its exercise, but also the conception of how much further it can be pushed.'' Bullock, *Hitler and Stalin,* 182.

29. Little is made, today, for example, of Herzl's intense love of Wagner, a love that was as much a part of his most ardent Zionist years as it was of his earlier assimilationist phase, or of his plan in *Der Judenstaat* for a modern industrialized Jewish state rather than the redemptively agrarian one so central to left-wing Zionist ideology after his death. More poignantly, the initial callousness of the 1930s Zionist leadership to reports of Nazi persecutions, a callousness that so shocks us today, arose in part because the extent and ferocity of the German attacks was simply not imaginable. Thus, when *Hapoel Hatsair* (the weekly newspaper of the Labor [Mapai] Party), in the March 21, 1933, issue, ''described the Nazi persecution of the Jews as 'punishment' for their having tried to integrate into German society instead of leaving for Palestine while it was still possible to do so,'' or when the Revisionist paper *Hazit Haam* editorialized on June 2, 1933, that ''the Jews of Germany are being persecuted now not despite their efforts to be part of their country, but because of those efforts,'' the model the authors of statements like these

had in mind was something much closer to a state-inspired pogrom than to systematic genocide. Only from the perspective of backshadowing can the Zionist leaders in 1933 be judged guilty of not fully comprehending the enormity of the catastrophe about to be unleashed on European Jewry, and recent studies that illustrate the "blindness" of the *yishuv*'s spokesmen [the Jewish community in Palestine] by citing public pronouncements from the early 1930s fail to understand that Zionism itself was unprepared for something as unprecedented as "the final solution." But ironically, only backshadowing allowed the same leaders to claim, after the early 1940s, that the death camps were the "inevitable" outcome of European anti-Semitism and hence served as "proof" of the accuracy of their historical predictions and redemptive ideology. (The quotations are taken from Tom Segev, *The Seventh Million: The Israelis and the Holocaust,* trans. Haim Watzman [New York: Hill and Wang, 1993], 10. Segev cites numerous similar statements from contemporary Zionist newspapers and political meetings in Palestine published during the first years of Nazi rule in Germany.)

30. Jacob Katz, "Was the Holocaust Predictable?" *Commentary,* vol. 59, no. 5 (May 1975): 41. See also Katz, *From Prejudice to Destruction: Anti-Semitism, 1700–1933* (Cambridge: Harvard University Press, 1980).

31. Katz, "Was the Holocaust Predictable?" 41.

32. E. P. Thompson, *The Making of the English Working Class* (New York: Vintage, 1966), 12.

33. Hannah Arendt, *The Origins of Totalitarianism* (New York: Harcourt, Brace, 1951), 44. For a sympathetic treatment of Arendt's changing attitudes toward European Jewry, anti-Semitism, and Zionism, see Elisabeth Young-Bruehl, *Hannah Arendt: For Love of the World* (New Haven: Yale University Press, 1982). It is curious that the most representative collection of Arendt's essays on both the Nazi genocide and Zionism has appeared in a two-volume German edition, *Essays und Kommentare,* much of which is made up of scattered pieces originally published in English: vol. 1, *Nach Auschwitz;* vol. 2, *Die Krise des Zionismus;* both volumes ed. Eike Geisel and Klaus Bittermann (Berlin: Edition Tiamat, 1989).

34. S. Y. Agnon, *Two Tales,* trans. Walter Lever (New York: Schocken, 1966), 22.

35. The annexation of Austria was accomplished de facto the moment German troops entered the country on March 12, 1938, and became "legal" as the result of a plebiscite held on April 10, 1938. For Berkeley's dismissal of Arendt and Zweig, see *Vienna and Its Jews,* 106. Stefan Zweig's famous description of Austria under Franz Joseph as "the Golden Age of Security.

Everything in our almost thousand-year old Austrian monarchy seemed based on permanency, and the State itself was the chief guarantor of this stability" (*The World of Yesterday,* trans. Cedar Paul and Eden Paul [London: Cassell, 1987], 13), is regularly mocked for its shortsightedness by backshadowing commentators. But when Zweig wrote these lines, not long before his suicide in exile in Brazil in 1942, he knew just how illusory that "permanency" was and how unwilling the new state would be to guarantee the "stability" of its Jewish population. (Even the mention of Austria's "almost thousand-year old monarchy" is a deliberate and ironic echo of Hitler's boast of founding a "thousand-year *Reich.*") Zweig's relationship to the Austria of the Habsburgs, and especially to the position of Jews within the empire, was characteristically complicated, but it was never one of naive complacency, and it was precisely to preempt the easy censure of backshadowing that he emphasized the reasons for general, as well as Jewish, optimism in pre-World War I Austria.

36. Danto, *Analytical Philosophy of History,* 13.

37. Jürgen Habermas, "A Review of Gadamer's *Truth and Method,*" in Fred R. Dallymayr and Thomas A. McCarthy, *Understanding and Social Inquiry* (Notre Dame: University of Notre Dame Press, 1977), 346. I owe the suggestion to look into Habermas's review of Gadamer, a review that is also full of references to Danto's *Analytical Philosophy of History,* to Lawrence S. Rainey of Yale University. My argument throughout these pages was sharpened by Rainey's comments on an early draft of this section, which appeared in *Modernism/Modernity,* vol. 1, no. 1 (January 1994).

38. Habermas, "Review of Gadamer's *Truth and Method,*" 348–49.

39. It is only fair to mention here that, as Lawrence Rainey suggested to me in a letter, in the logic of Habermas's oeuvre as whole, he is primarily concerned with the legitimacy of a kind of "counterfactual backshadowing" (Rainey's term) intended to secure the critical potential of the utopian imagination. According to this view, in Habermas's writings, backshadowing is essentially counterfactual, and thus closer to my own position than it is to Danto's. But even Rainey agrees that the simplistic model of narrative and storytelling posited by both Habermas and Danto reinforces, even if unintentionally, precisely the kind of reductive historiographical backshadowing whose effects I criticize.

40. Wilhelm Dilthey, *Der Aufbau der geschichtlichen Welt in den Geisteswissenschaften,* in *Gesammelte Schriften* 3:233. Quoted in Habermas, "Review of Gadamer's *Truth and Method,*" 350–51.

41. My argument here is, of course, not intended to deny the importance

of messianic thinking in the Jewish tradition. But Jewish thought has usually conceived of the significance of the messianic, and more specifically, the relationship between the messianic moment and ordinary time, in a different way than does Christianity. For Jews, the Messiah's coming does not automatically minimize, let alone negate, the value of daily activities in the world. For example, there is a famous Talmudic story about a man who is planting a tree when he hears that the Messiah has arrived. The fascinating conclusion of the debate about what he ought to do next is that his obligation is first to complete the planting of the tree and only then to go and see the Messiah. See Hayim Nahman Bialik and Yehoshua Hana Ravnitzky, eds., *The Book of Legends: Sefer Ha-Aggadah,* trans. William G. Braude (New York: Schocken, 1992), 361. Even in the direct physical presence of the transcendent, one's responsibilities toward the regular, normative world are not suspended; the messianic impulse in Judaism is rarely a form of judgment in whose light nothing else has any importance. In many strains of Christian thinking, however, the world is only the site of a pilgrimage intended to prepare one for eternity, and the actions performed in the world ultimately count only insofar as they are the grounds of the judgment that decides one's eternal destiny. (So, for example, in *Purgatorio* 5, Dante shows us that a man like Buonconte da Montefeltro could spend his life engaged in violence, but the sincerity of his last minute repentance suffices to gain his salvation.)

42. On Schönerer's career both before and after the attack on the *Neues Wiener Tageblatt,* see Carl Schorske's *Fin-De-Siècle Vienna: Politics and Culture* (New York: Knopf, 1980). For a respectful, but I think fundamental, critique of some of Schorske's major assumptions, see Steven Beller, *Vienna and the Jews, 1867–1938: A Cultural History* (Cambridge: Cambridge University Press, 1989). The best brief account of the differences between Schönerer and Lueger, and of Lueger's increasing conservatism and rapprochement with the propertied classes once he was confirmed as mayor, see Robert S. Wistrich, *The Jews of Vienna in the Age of Franz Joseph* (Oxford: Oxford University Press, 1989), especially the chapter called "The New Austrian Anti-Semitism," 205–37.

43. Ignatieff, "Rise and Fall of Vienna's Jews," 22.

44. For a fascinating discussion of the link between Nazi rhetoric and imagery and that of Schönerer's movement, see Jean-Pierre Faye, *Langages totalitaires* (Paris: Hermann, 1972). Steven Beller says that while "Schönerer's brand of racial antisemitism . . . never posed a serious threat to Austria's Jews . . . [it] was very powerful at exactly the most crucial point, as far as Jews in

the cultural élite were concerned, in the student body of the German university—the group of future teachers and officials." Beller, *Vienna and the Jews,* 192.

45. Theodor Herzl, *Briefe und Tagebücher,* ed. Alex Bein, Hermann Grieve, Moshe Schaerf, and Julius Schoeps, 4 vols. (Frankfurt: Ullstein/Propyläen, 1983), 2:252:

> Gegen Abend ging ich auf die Landstrasse. Vor dem Wahlhaus eine stumm aufgeregte Menge. Plötzlich kam Dr.Lueger heraus auf den Platz. Begeisterte Hochrufe, aus den Fenstern schwenkten Frauen weisse Tücher. Die Polizei hielt die Leute zurück. Neben mir sagte Einer mit zärtlicher Wärme aber in stillem Ton: "Das ist unser Führer!" Mehr eigentlich als alle Deklamationen und Schimpfereien hat mir dieses Wort gezeigt wie tief der Antisemitismus in den Herzen dieser Bevölkerung wurzelt."
>
> (Toward evening, I walked along the Landstrasse. In front of the polling station, a silently excited crowd. All of a sudden, Dr. Lueger emerged onto the square. Rousing cheers, women waving white sheets out of the windows. The police held the people back. [Someone standing] next to me said with tender warmth but in a calm tone: "That is our Führer." This expression, more than any other declamations and revilings, showed me how deeply anti-Semitism was rooted in this population.)

46. For a powerful recent treatment of the legacy of Hitler's triumphant entry into Vienna on March 15, 1938, see Thomas Bernhard's play, *Heldenplatz* (Frankfurt: Suhrkamp, 1989).

47. Lang, *Act and Idea in the Nazi Genocide,* 195.

48. Even Herzl does not seem to have been overly worried about Schönerer's legacy or influence. He certainly saw Schönerer as a characteristic example of Austrian anti-Semitism, but in the *Letters* and *Diaries* there are surprisingly few references to him, and when Schönerer's name does appear, it is usually as one of a long list of dangerous political leaders. One typical entry in 1895 (*Briefe und Tagebücher* 2:113) records a dream in which Herzl sees himself challenging either Schönerer, Lueger, or Aloys Prinz von Liechtenstein (1846–1920; a chief voice of the reactionary party in the Austrian Reichstag, successful anti-Semitic candidate, and ally of Lueger in the Christian-Social Party) to a duel:

> Einer meiner Träume der unklaren Zeit war: Alois Lichtenstein, Schönerer oder Lueger zum Duell zwingen. Wäre ich erschossen worden, hätte mein hinterlassener Brief der Welt gesagt, dass ich als Opfer der ungerechtesten Bewegung fiel. So möge mein Tod wenigstens die Köpfe und Herzen der Menschen bessern. Hätte ich aber den Gegner erschossen, so wollte ich vor dem Schwurgerichte eine grossartige Rede halten, worin ich zuerst ,,den Tod

eines Ehrenmannes" bedauerte. . . . Dann wäre ich auf die Judenfrage ein-
gegangen, hätte eine gewaltige Lassalle'sche Rede gehalten, die Geschwornen
erschüttert, gerührt, dem Gerichtshof Achtung abgezwungen—und wäre frei-
gesprochen worden.

(One of the dreams I had during the time of my confusion [i.e., before
the discovery of Zionism as a life-goal], was to compel Alois Lichtenstein,
Schönerer, or Lueger to a duel. If I had been shot, the letter I would have
left behind would have announced to the world that I had fallen victim to
one of the most unjust of all movements [anti-Semitism]. At least in this way
my death would have improved the minds and the hearts of the people. However, had I shot my adversary, I would have given a grand speech in front of
the jury, in which I would have first regretted "the death of an honorable
man." . . . Subsequently, I would have turned to the Jewish question: I would
have delivered a powerful speech in the style of Lassalle, stirred up and moved
the jury, forced them into paying me respect—and then I would have been
acquitted.)

49. George Clare, *Last Waltz in Vienna: The Destruction of a Family, 1842–
1942* (London: Macmillan 1981), 121; first published as *Das waren die Klaars*
(Berlin: Verlag Ullstein, 1980).

50. Ibid., 186.

51. Langer, *Holocaust Testimonies*, 29.

52. Emmanuel Berl, *Interrogatoire par Patrick Modiano suivi de Il fait beau,
allons au Cimetière* (Paris: Gallimard, 1976).

53. Arthur Schnitzler, *Der Weg ins Freie* (Frankfurt: S. Fischer Verlag,
1978). The translation by Horace Samuel, *The Road to the Open* (New York:
Knopf, 1923) has recently been reprinted with a useful new foreword by
William M. Jonston (Evanston, Ill.: Northwestern University Press, 1991). My
quotations in the text are taken from this edition, with the original German
provided in the notes. In 1992 the University of California Press published
a new English version, called *The Road into the Open,* translated by Roger
Byers with an introduction by Russell A. Berman. The sudden and almost
simultaneous availability of two translations indicates that Schnitzler's novel
is coming to be considered among the most important works of its period,
especially for anyone interested in the question of Jewish life and consciousness in fin-de-siècle Vienna. For helpful discussions of the historical background to *Der Weg ins Freie,* see the chapter "Arthur Schnitzler's Road to the
Open," in Wistrich, *Jews of Vienna in the Age of Franz Joseph,* 583–620; Wistrich's
earlier essay "Arthur Schnitzler's 'Jewish Problem,' " *The Jewish Quarterly,*
vol. 22, no. 4 (Winter 1975), 27–30; and Harry Zohn, "Three Austrian Jews
in German Literature: Schnitzler, Zweig, Herzl," in Josef Fraenkel, ed., *The*

Jews of Austria: Essays on Their Life, History, and Destruction (London: Vallentine, Mitchell, 1967), 67–82.

54. Schnitzler, *Der Weg ins Freie* (Northwestern University Press ed., 250).

Glauben Sie, daß es einen Christen auf Erden gibt, und wäre es der edelste, gerechteste und treueste, einen einzigen, der nicht in irgendeinem Augenblick des Grolls, des Unmuts, des Zorns selbst gegen seinen besten Freund, gegen seine Geliebte, gegen seine Frau, wenn sie Juden oder jüdischer Abkunft waren, deren Judentum, innerlich wenigstens, ausgespielt hätte? Was sie Verfolgungswahnsinn zu nennen belieben, lieber Georg, das ist eben in Wahrheit nichts anderes als ein ununterbrochen waches, sehr intensives Wissen von einem Zustand, in dem wir Juden uns befinden, und viel eher als von Verfolgungswahnsinn könnte man von einem Wahn des Geborgenseins, des Inruhegelassenwerdens reden, von einem Sicherheitswahn, der vielleicht eine minder auffallende, aber für den Befallenen viel gefährlichere Krankheitsform vorstellt. (Fischer ed., 203–4).

55. Ibid. (Northwestern University Press ed.), 107–10.

'Mein Instinkt . . . sagt mir untrüglich, daß hier, gerade hier meine Heimat ist und nicht in irgend einem Land, das ich nicht kenne, das mir nach den Schilderungen nicht im geringsten zusagt und das mir gewisse Leute jetzt als Vaterland einreden wollen, mit der Begründung, daß meine Urahnen vor einigen tausend Jahren gerade von dort aus in die Welt verstreut worden sind.' . . . Nationalgefühl und Religionen, das waren seit jeher Worte, die . . . ihn erbitterten. . . . Und was die Religionen anbelangte, so ließ er sich christliche und jüdische Legenden so gut gefallen, als hellenische und indische; aber jede war ihm gleich unerträglich und widerlich, wenn sie ihm ihre Dogmen aufzudrängen suchte. . . . Und am wenigsten würde ihn je das Bewußtsein gemeinsam erlittener Verfolgung, gemeinsam lastenden Hasses mit Menschen verbinden, denen er sich innerlich fern fühle. Als moralisches Prinzip und als Wohlfahrtsaktion wollte er den Zionismus gelten lassen, . . . die Idee einer Errichtung des Judenstaates auf religiöser und nationaler Grundlage erscheine ihm wie eine unsinnige Auflehnung gegen den Geist aller geschichtlichen Entwicklung. (Fischer ed., 92–93)

56. On this theme, see Sander L. Gilman, *Jewish Self-Hatred: Anti-Semitism and the Hidden Language of the Jews* (Baltimore: Johns Hopkins University Press, 1986). Although I disagree with several of Gilman's premises and believe that in general the explanatory force of "Jewish self-hatred" has been greatly overestimated, Gilman's study is a serious attempt to understand the phenomenon, and it does not fall into the easy clichés with which backshadowing burdens Jewish history. But given the carelessness with which the phrase is used, there may be some advantage to using Hermann Broch's less familiar term "inner anti-Semitism." Nonetheless, for all my reservations, I

have no doubt that some form of what we call "Jewish self-hatred" did exist, although more among the families of converted, rather than secularized, Jews. Indeed, one of the most discouraging examples that I have come across only became fully known after Gilman's book was published. In Ray Monk's biography, *Ludwig Wittgenstein: The Duty of Genius* (New York: Free Press, 1990), there are unmistakable indications that Wittgenstein had internalized many of the most pernicious myths about Jews current in the Vienna of his youth, and in moments of doubt applied them all to himself. These even included the notion of the Jew in European history "as a sort of disease [that] no one wants to put ... on the same level as normal life ... [and to which no one can grant] the same rights as healthy bodily processes." (314). Monk comments how truly sad it is to see that

> just as Wittgenstein was beginning to develop an entirely new method for tackling philosophical problems—a method that has no precedent in the entire tradition of Western philosophy ... he should be inclined to assess his own philosophical contribution within the framework of the absurd charge that the Jew was incapable of original thought. "It is typical for a Jewish mind," he wrote, "to understand someone else's work better than [that person] understands it himself." Wittgenstein describes his own work, for example, as essentially nothing more than a clarification of other people's ideas:
>
> > Amongst Jews "genius" is found only in the holy man. Even the greatest of Jewish thinkers is no more than talented. (Myself for instance.) I think there is some truth in my idea that I really only think reproductively. I don't believe I have ever *invented* a line of thinking. I have always taken over from someone else. I have simply straightaway seized on it with enthusiasm for my work of clarification. That is how Boltzmann, Hertz, Schopenhauer, Frege, Russell, Kraus, Loos, Weininger, Spengler, Sraffa have influenced me. Can one take the case of Breuer and Freud as an example of Jewish reproductiveness?— What I invent are new *similes.* (316–17)

57. John Dewey, *Logic: The Theory of Inquiry* (New York: H. Holt, 1938), 239.

58. The first text that I know of in which the actual phrase "a usable past" occurs is Van Wyck Brooks, "On Creating a Usable Past," *The Dial,* vol. 64, no. 764 (April 11, 1918): 337–41. Since its initial formulation in the work of writers like Dewey, Beard, and Brooks, the concept has been attacked as tendentious and ahistorical, without however, ceasing to exert its own counter-pressure on more conventional notions of historiography. See especially Arthur O. Lovejoy, "Present Standpoints and Past History," *Journal of Philosophy,* vol. 36, no. 18 (August 1939): 477–89; and Ernest Nagel, "Some Issues in the Logic of Historical Analysis," *Scientific Monthly* 74 (March 1952): 162–69.

59. Walter Benjamin, "Theses on the Philosophy of History," in his *Illuminations,* ed. Hannah Arendt, trans. Harry Zohn (New York: Schocken, 1969), 255.

60. Ernst Pawel, *The Labyrinth of Exile: A Life of Theodor Herzl* (New York: Farrar, Strauss and Giroux, 1989), 61.

61. Ibid., 358.

62. It is worth pointing out, though, that debates about the proper relationship with the Arabs were always an important part of the internal struggles in Zionist ideology, as the early quarrels between Ahad Ha-Am and Herzl make clear. The controversy about the actual number and location of Arabs in Turkish, and then in Mandate, Palestine continues to be a fiercely controversial and partisan topic in current historical/demographic studies of the region. For a penetrating biography of Herzl's most important opponent in the Zionist movement, who openly rejected Herzl's optimistic assessment of future Arab-Jewish relationships, see Steven J. Zipperstein, *Elusive Prophet: Ahad Ha'am and the Origins of Zionism* (Berkeley and Los Angeles: University of California Press, 1993).

3. NARRATING THE SHOAH

1. Theodor W. Adorno, "Engagement," in *Noten zur Literatur, Gesammelte Schriften* (Frankfurt: Suhrkamp, 1974), 2:423:

> Die sogenannte künstlerische Gestaltung des nackten körperlichen Schmerzes der mit Gewehrkolben Niedergeknüppelten enthält, sei's noch so entfernt, das Potential, Genuß herauszupressen. Die Moral, die der Kunst gebietet, es keine Sekunde zu vergessen, schliddert in den Abgrund ihres Gegenteils. Durchs ästhetische Stilisationsprinzip, und gar das feierliche Gebet des Chors, erscheint das unausdenkliche Schicksal doch, als hätte es irgend Sinn gehabt; es wird verklärt, etwas von dem Grauen weggenommen; damit allein schon widerfährt den Opfern Unrecht.

A more nuanced and provocative account of Adorno's sentences would emphasize not so much the *reader's* pleasure, but *literature's* own self-delight, the inevitable accents of mastery and joy in its expressive powers that all great art exhibits, irrespective of the immediate theme. From this perspective, what appalls Adorno is not the failure of literature to be adequate to the demands of its subject but, on the contrary, its limitless capacity to transform anything, including the death camps, into an "occasion" for the display of its potency. For a searching reaction to this problem in the light of our contemporary fascination with "poetry of witness," see John Bayley, "Night Train," *New York Review of Books*, vol. 40, no. 12 (June 24, 1993): 20–22.

2. Leo Bersani, *The Culture of Redemption* (Cambridge: Harvard University Press, 1990), 1.

3. Fackenheim then spells out the implications of his commandment as follows: "We are first commanded to survive as Jews, lest the Jewish people perish. We are commanded, second, to remember in our very guts and bones the martyrs of the Holocaust, lest their memory perish. We are forbidden, thirdly, to deny or despair of God, however much we may have to contend with him or believe in him, lest Judaism perish. We are forbidden, finally, to despair of the world as the place which is to become the kingdom of God, lest we help make it a meaningless place in which God is dead or irrelevant and everything is permitted. To abandon any of these imperatives, in response to Hitler's victory at Auschwitz, would be to hand him yet other, posthumous victories." This injunction was originally delivered during the symposium "Jewish Values in the Post-Holocaust Future," held in New York City on March 26, 1967. It was subsequently published under the title "The 614th Commandment" in *Judaism*, vol. 16, no. 3 (Summer 1967): 269–73, and has been reprinted in Fackenheim's collection of essays, *The Jewish Return into History: Reflections in the Age of Auschwitz and a New Jerusalem* (New York: Schocken, 1978), 19–24.

4. *Muselmänner* (literally, "Muslims") is the term coined in the concentration camps for those "near-skeletons who, their feelings, thoughts, and even speech already murdered by hunger and torture, still walked for a while till they dropped to the ground." See Emil Fackenheim, *To Mend the World* (New York: Schocken, 1982), xix.

5. Primo Levi, *The Drowned and the Saved*, trans. Raymond Rosenthal (New York: Summit Books, 1988), 11. Levi attributes the story to "the last pages" of Simon Wiesenthal's *The Murderers Are Among Us*, but this must be a faulty recollection since Wiesenthal's account is significantly different. Wiesenthal remembers being asked by SS Rottenführer (Corporal) Merz, " 'Suppose an eagle took you to America. . . . What would you tell them there?' " After being repeatedly assured that he would not be punished for telling the truth, Wiesenthal told Merz, " 'I believe I would tell the people the truth.' " But to this, Merz calmly replied, " 'You would tell the truth to the people in America. That's right. And you know what would happen, Wiesenthal? . . . They wouldn't believe you. They'd say you were crazy. Might even put you in a madhouse. How can *anyone* believe this terrible business—unless he

has lived through it?' " Simon Wiesenthal, *The Murderers Are Among Us,* ed. Joseph Wechsberg (New York: McGraw-Hill, 1967), 334–35.

6. Himmler's speech is printed as "Document 1919-PS" in volume 19 of the *Trial of the Major War Criminals Before the International Military Tribunal: Nuremberg, 14 November 1945–1 October 1946* (New York: AMS Press, 1948), 110–173. The passages cited are on page 145 of the transcript. A partial translation of Himmler's talk can be found in Lucy T. Dawidowicz, ed., *A Holocaust Reader* (New York: Behrman House, 1976), 130–40. For a fine analysis of the speech, see Peter Haidu, "The Dialectics of Unspeakability: Language, Silence, and the Narratives of Desubjectification," in Saul Friedlander, ed., *Probing the Limits of Representation: Nazism and the "Final Solution"* (Cambridge: Harvard University Press, 1992), 277–99.

7. Levi, *Drowned and the Saved,* 83–84: "We survivors are not only an exiguous but also an anomalous minority: we are those who by their prevarications or abilities or good luck did not touch bottom. Those who did so, those who saw the Gorgon, have not returned to tell about it or have returned mute, but they are the 'Muslims,' the submerged, the complete witnesses, the ones whose depositions would have a general significance."

8. Primo Levi, *The Drowned and the Saved,* 19.

9. Tom Segev, *The Seventh Million: The Israelis and the Holocaust* (New York: Hill and Wang, 1993), 8.

10. Helen Lewis, *A Time to Speak* (Belfast: Blackstaff, 1992), Foreword by Jennifer Johnston, ix.

11. Already before the Israeli Supreme Court ruling, District Judge Thomas A. Wiseman Jr., reviewing the case for the U.S. Sixth Court of Appeals, concluded in June 1993 that new evidence, largely from the secret police files of the former U.S.S.R., exculpated Demjanjuk from the "specific crimes" of Ivan the Terrible.

12. James E. Young, *Writing and Rewriting the Holocaust: Narrative Consequences of Interpretation* (Bloomington: Indiana University Press, 1988), 26, 31.

13. Jonathan Boyarin, *Storm from Paradise: The Politics of Jewish Memory* (Minneapolis: University of Minnesota Press, 1992), 86.

14. Dominick LaCapra, "The Personal, the Political, and the Textual: Paul de Man as Object of Transference," *History and Memory,* vol. 4, no. 1 (Spring/Summer 1992): 15.

15. Thomas Keneally, *Schindler's List* (New York: Simon and Schuster, 1982), 10. These examples were suggested to me by Berel Lang, *Act and Idea in the Nazi Genocide* (Chicago: University of Chicago Press, 1990), 133ff.

16. Berel Lang, ed., *Writing and the Holocaust* (New York: Holmes and Meier, 1988), 4–6.

17. Lang, *Act and Idea in the Nazi Genocide,* 135.

18. George Steiner, "The Long Life of Metaphor: An Approach to the Shoah," in Lang, ed., *Writing and the Holocaust,* 160.

19. Aharon Appelfeld, quoted in Lang, ed., *Writing and the Holocaust,* 83.

20. Henri Raczymow, "La mémoire trouée," *Pardès* 3 (1986): 180: "De quel droit parler, si l'on n'a été, comme c'est mon cas, ni victime, ni rescapé, ni témoin de l'événement?" The entire issue of *Pardès,* on the topic "Paris-Jerusalem—Les Juifs de France: Aventure personnelle ou destin collectif?" is extraordinarily interesting and inflects the issues we have been debating here with the singular perspectives of the contemporary Franco-Jewish intelligentsia. In English, see Ellen S. Fine's helpful essay "The Absent Memory: The Act of Writing in Post-Holocaust French Literature," in Lang, ed., *Writing and the Holocaust,* 41–57. My own interest in Raczymow was initially stimulated by Fine's sensitive discussion of his work.

21. Henri Raczymow, *Un Cri sans voix* (Paris: Gallimard, 1985), 186: "Je ne vois rien. . . . Je ne veux rien voir. Vouloir voir me placerait du côté du S.S. chargé de voir par l'oeilleton de la chambre à gaz l'état des gazés."

22. Norma Rosen, "The Second Life of Holocaust Imagery" *Midstream,* vol. 33, no. 4 (April 1987): 58.

23. Ibid., 58.

24. See the interview with A. B. Yehoshua in Joseph Cohen, *Voices of Israel: Essays on and Interviews with Yehuda Amichai, A. B. Yehoshua, T. Carmi, Aharon Appelfeld, and Amos Oz* (Albany: SUNY Press, 1990), 74, 77. See also Sidra DeKoven Ezrahi's analysis of this pattern as necessary for Israeli self-consciousness. She calls it "the slow but ideologically consistent process by which, in the decades after the war, the Holocaust was assimilated into the logic of Jewish regeneration so that it would not shake the foundations of the new state." Ezrahi, "Considering the Apocalypse: Is the Writing on the Wall Only Graffiti?" in Lang, ed., *Writing and the Holocaust,* 137–53; and "Revisioning the Past: The Changing Legacy of the Holocaust in Hebrew Literature," *Salmagundi,* nos. 68–69 (Fall 1985–Winter 1986: 245–70). As is clear from the arguments in this section, I am inherently suspicious of the appeal to *raison d'état* in such a context, but at the descriptive, if not justificatory, level I find the specific details of Ezrahi's argument fascinating. Nonetheless, one of the things that makes the earlier silence more like an act of repression than a "slow but ideologically consistent process" is that when, in large part triggered by the Eichmann trial and then reinforced by the

trauma of the 1973 Yom Kippur War, it became impossible to continue avoiding a confrontation with the Shoah, that confrontation followed so powerfully the psychoanalytic logic of the "return of the repressed." The topic flooded the national consciousness, until in Saul Friedlander's description, "There are today more books in Israel about the Shoah than about probably any event in Israel's history." From a roundtable discussion printed in Lang, ed., *Writing and the Holocaust*, 288.

25. Freema Gottlieb, "A Talk with Aharon Appelfeld," *New York Times Book Review*, November 23, 1980, p. 42.

26. Yael S. Feldman, "Whose Story Is It Anyway: Ideology and Psychology in the Representation of the Shoah in Israeli Literature," in Friedlander, ed., *Probing the Limits of Representation*, 229.

27. Tom Segev has shown how many of the most influential Zionist writers continued to maintain a punitive judgmental tone about European Jewry, even after the news of the death camps became widespread in the *yishuv*. Thus, for example, on November 27, 1942, "*Davar* [the left-wing daily paper of the Histadrut Labor Federation] published an article describing the extermination of the Jews as 'punishment from heaven for not having come to Palestine.' " Segev, *Seventh Million*, 98. In addition to the demoralizing tone blaming the victims for their fate, there is the absurdity of invoking "heaven" by an anti-religious, secular movement in order to add a still greater weight to the relentlessness of its historical self-confidence.

28. Esther Fuchs, "Author with a Dual Root: An Interview with Itamar Yaoz-Kest," a chapter in Fuchs, *Encounters with Israeli Authors* (Marblehead, Mass.: Micah Publications, 1982), 29. Appelfeld calls this strain in Zionism "a piece of wishful thinking. It tried to impose the peasant as the Jewish norm and cut itself off from the old Jewish typology of an uprooted people. . . . The Zionist wish to create a 'normal' society . . . does not take into consideration the greatness, as well as the flaws, of the old pattern. Though the early Zionist may have hoped to escape from the Jewish fate, one cannot escape from oneself, and should not really want to." Gottlieb, "Talk with Aharon Appelfeld," 42.

29. Segev, *Seventh Million*, 179.

30. Cohen, *Voices of Israel*, 138.

31. Alan Mintz, *Hurban: Responses to Catastrophe in Hebrew Literature* (New York: Columbia University Press, 1984), 204. Mintz goes on to empasize that the word for rescue itself, *hatsalah*, meant not just bringing the survivors to *Eretz Israel* but rehabilitating and "redeeming" them, which included having them forget the past. (243).

32. Segev, *Seventh Million,* 158. The strength of the *yishuv*'s desire to shed any signs of Diaspora weakness is evident even at the most basic level of speech. As Benjamin Harshav's *The Meaning of Yiddish* (Berkeley and Los Angeles: University of California Press, 1990), 132, points out, "The 'Sephardic'[North African] pronunciation adopted in Israeli Hebrew, with its strong, 'masculine' stress on the last syllable of each word, was the symbol of virility and determination as opposed to the whining 'oy' and 'ay' of Ashkenazi [European] Hebrew." That this decision was made largely by Ashkenazi Jews who continued to look down on Sephardic ones as culturally inferior is not the smallest irony in the complex issue of Jewish self-transformation in its Zionist version.

33. In a 1986 interview, Appelfeld protested against his reputation in the minds of English-speaking readers as the author of novels about the assimilated Jews in the Shoah: "I've published ten novels and five collections of short stories in Hebrew plus a volume of essays. There are many other manuscripts in progress. The five novels translated and published in America thus far happen to deal with assimilated Jews. . . . But they are not my only Jewish subjects. . . . I am also working on stories of Jewish life in eastern Europe sixty or seventy years ago. And I have done three novels on the lives of Jews living in the Middle Ages." Cohen, *Voices of Israel,* 133. Yet in the same collection of interviews, Yehuda Amichai, A. B. Yehoshua, and Amos Oz all refer to Appelfeld as notable primarily for his portrait of the world of assimilated Austro-German Jewry on the eve of the Shoah, so irrespective of the quantitative injustice of such a judgment, it clearly echoes more than merely the accidents of translation into English.

34. Robert Alter, "Mother and Son, Lost in a Continent," *New York Times Book Review,* November 2, 1986, pp. 1, 34–35.

35. On this theme, see Steven E. Aschheim, *Brothers and Strangers: The East European Jew in German and German Jewish Consciousness, 1800–1923* (Madison: University of Wisconsin Press, 1983).

36. Austrian Jews had long been in the habit of vacationing at resorts that were *Judenfreundlich* [hospitable to Jews], less out of any particular "clannishness" or desire to remain exclusively among their own kind, than as a consequence of being barred from numerous other spas. George Berkeley quotes a proclamation by the mayor of Maria Tafel, one of these spa towns, issued in July, 1920: "It has been repeatedly observed that Jews are finding lodgings and meals in Maria Tafel. Owners of hotels, coffee houses, and inns are requested not to cater to Jews. . . . Maria Tafel is the most famous health resort in Lower Austria and not a Jewish temple." Berkeley adds that "an-

other resort community, Erfinding, decreed that no Jew could stay in the town for more than twenty-four hours." Berkeley, *Vienna and Its Jews: The Tragedy of Success* (Cambridge, Mass.: Madison Books / Abt Books, 1989), 158.) In 1922, in order to be permitted to stay overnight in the resort town of Mattsee, near Salzburg, Arnold Schoenberg was asked to produce a certificate of baptism to counter charges that he was a Jew. Although Schoenberg had converted to Lutheranism in 1898, the incident at Mattsee, along with others of a similar character, acted as a catalyst for the composer's return to Judaism. Robert S. Wistrich, *The Jews of Vienna in the Age of Franz Joseph* (Oxford: Oxford University Press, 1989), 630–32. Thus, no matter how assimilationist, or how eager to deny their identities, long before the date of the novel's actions, vacationers in a place like Badenheim would have been sufficiently conscious of being Jews to have chosen (or been indirectly forced) to go to a resort that was ready to accept them. Moreover, Appelfeld is fully aware of these details and freely uses them in his other novels. *The Age of Wonders*, for example, opens with the twelve-year-old narrator's memory of when he and his mother were suddenly expelled from the vacation resort where they were spending the summer of 1938 by anti-Semitic pressure.

37. Aharon Appelfeld, *Badenheim 1939*, trans. Dalya Bilu (Boston: David R. Godine, 1980), 147. Future references are to this edition and are acknowledged in the body of the text.

38. Gabriel Josipovici, "Silently Mending," *Times Literary Supplement*, November 19, 1982, p. 1269. Josipovici makes his comment in a review of Appelfeld's *The Age of Wonders*, but his description applies equally to *Badenheim 1939*, both in its accuracy and in its blindness to how Appelfeld actually achieves his commendable discretion.

39. For a powerful, but I think finally unpersuasive, statement of the opposite point of view, see Philip Roth's justification for Appelfeld's strategy: "In your books, there's no news from the public realm that might serve as a warning to an Appelfeld victim, nor is the victim's impending doom presented as part of a European catastrophe. The historical focus is supplied by the reader, who understands, as the victims cannot, the magnitude of the enveloping evil. Your reticence as a historian, when combined with the historical perspective of a knowing reader, accounts for the peculiar impact your work has—for the power that emanates from the stories that are told through such very modest means. Also, dehistoricizing the events and blurring the background, you probably approximate the disorientation felt by

people who were unaware that they were on the brink of a cataclysm." Philip Roth, "A Talk with Aharon Appelfeld," *New York Times Book Review,* February 28, 1988, p. 28.

40. Thomas Flanagan, " 'We Have Not Far To Go' " *The Nation,* January 31, 1981, p. 122.

41. See, for example, Irving Howe, "Novels of Other Times and Places," *New York Times Book Review,* November 23, 1980, pp. 1, 40–41.

42. Appelfeld himself has emphasized a spiritual affinity with Kafka, both the fiction writer and the diarist, and admirers like Philip Roth have stressed the pertinence of an Appelfeld-Kafka connection. Roth, "Talk with Aharon Appelfeld," 1, 28. It seems to me, however, that Kafka actually *underdetermines* the meanings and emotional resonance of a story, thereby making it hauntingly (re)interpretable as the reader is driven to work out its significance in new contexts. But the central place of the Shoah in Appelfeld's fiction, its function as a kind of negative sublime exceeding representation but drawing all of the local meanings into its darkness, has precisely the opposite effect from Kafka's uncanny openness to contradictory readings.

43. Idris Parry considers these similes as part of Appelfeld's technique of showing us "people who will believe what they want to believe, not what the evidence suggests," and aptly describes the novel's scenes as "created like a series of sharp perspectives in a model theatre." Parry, "The Voices of Sickness," *Times Literary Supplement,* November 20, 1981, p. 1374.

44. Stefan Zweig, *The World of Yesterday,* trans. Cedar Paul and Eden Paul (London: Cassell, 1987), 285. For an Italian parallel to the theme of Jews deliberately ignoring a tightening net of anti-Semitic decrees, see Giorgio Bassani's masterful novel, *Il Giardino dei Finzi-Contini* (Torino: Einaudi, 1962), translated into English by Isabel Quigly as *The Garden of the Finzi-Continis* (London: Faber and Faber, 1965).

45. George Clare, *Last Waltz in Vienna: The Destruction of a Family, 1842–1942* (London: Macmillan, 1981), 154.

46. It is only fair to point out that even in *Badenheim 1939* there are occasional glimpses that a more complex and nuanced relationship to the characters is imaginable by the narrator. Apparitions like the old rabbi who suddenly materializes in the town just before the mass deportations, or the emaciated twins who present uncannily ritualistic recitations of Rilke, come close to being figures of sufficient resonance to elicit the kind of solicitude and affective sympathy that the rest of the novel is reluctant to provide. But in his very integrity, the rabbi serves principally to make evident how far the

vacationers have strayed from any contact with Jewish tradition, while the twins' performance represents the kind of spiritually, and ultimately, physically self-destructive fascination that Austro-German high culture held for educated Jews. Nowhere does Appelfeld's sympathy, even when it alights on a particular character, bring with it a noticeable mitigation of his contempt for the decisions, daily habits, and cultural values of the assimilated Austro-Jewish community.

47. See Berkeley, *Vienna and Its Jews,* 266–97, for a description of Eichmann's methods and a tabulation of Jewish emigration from Austria. Norman Bentwich, who was the Attorney General for Palestine from 1920 to 1931, was in Vienna in the days of the *Anschluss* and has written a vivid account of "the savagery, the persecution, and the despair" with which the community was stricken. He describes "the vast queues that gathered outside the consulates of possible 'host' countries: the United States, South America, the United Kingdom, France, Belgium, Holland. The queues stretched for miles and were subject to constant attack." Bentwich, "The Destruction of the Jewish Community in Austria, 1938–1942," in Josef Fraenkel, ed., *The Jews of Austria: Essays on their Life, History, and Destruction* (London: Vallentine, Mitchell, 1967), 468.

48. The number of Austrian Jews granted visas by other countries is shockingly small: Britain let in 31,000 and another 9,000 reached safety in British Palestine; the United States admitted just over 28,000, China 18,000, Belgium over 4,000, Australia and New Zealand together 1,900, and Canada 82. (These figures are cited in Berkeley, *Vienna and Its Jews,* 282.) One of the most detailed, and depressing studies of the reluctance of the United States to do anything to help Europe's Jews is David S. Wyman, *The Abandonment of the Jews: America and the Holocaust, 1941–1945* (New York: Pantheon, 1984).

49. In one of his best stories, "1946," Appelfeld has a wonderful argument between two survivors temporarily sheltered in a Displaced Person's Camp in southern Italy in which the failure of assimilation is acknowledged, but the blame for it is put on the Aryans, not the Jews. Against this view is a kind of simple-man's, homespun, Fackenheim-like argument that only a return to traditional Jewish religious custom can make sense after the Shoah has made clear the catastrophic failure of other paths: " 'An assimilationist is what I am—an assimilationist born and bred.' 'Your success has been rather limited, if you don't mind my saying so.' 'Correct, but through no fault of my own. I did what was required of an assimilationist. . . . You would like me to proclaim to the world that assimilation has failed. From now on,

every assimilationist will put on phylacteries and pray every morning.' 'That would be an honorable position of a sort, in my opinion.' " "1946" trans. Dalya Bilu, *Jerusalem Quarterly*, no.7 (Spring 1978): 127. In many ways, "1946" can be read as a kind of inverse *Badenheim 1939*, but without the later novel's allegorical structure or coolly mocking narrative tone. "1946" is a prosaically realistic tale with a complex and variegated set of characters. The story concerns a group of Jews who survived the Shoah primarily by hiding in the forests of eastern Europe and are now waiting to get to Australia or, if necessary (since many of them are reluctant to go there), to Palestine. Perhaps because it is set after the genocide and thus is "narratable," Appelfeld can let himself describe different types of Jews more convincingly than in his pre-Shoah settings. Nothing in "1946" serves as a warning or a prefiguration of future events, and its irony (about Zionism as well as assimilationism) is fully earned by the characters' own behavior. The story even ends with the arrival of the ship that will take them all to Palestine, as part of the still illegal *aliyah,* thus exactly paralleling, but in a positive sense, the train awaiting the vacationers at the end of *Badenheim 1939.*

50. Friedlander, ed., *Probing the Limits of Representation*, 16.

51. Ruth R. Wisse, "Aharon Appelfeld, Survivor," *Commentary*, vol. 76, no. 2 (August 1983): 74–76.

52. I owe this phrase to a subtle, if ultimately hostile reading of this chapter by an anonymous reviewer for the journal *Common Knowledge.*

53. This motif is so central to Appelfeld's vision of Austro-German Jewry that it figures in almost every one of his novels on the theme. As an example, consider the similarity between the passage from *Badenheim 1939* quoted in the text and the following formulation from *The Age of Wonders* (trans. Dalya Bilu [Boston: David R. Godine, 1981], 163–64): "Since nobody knew that these were the last days in this house, on this street, and behind the grid of this lattice . . . since nobody knew, everyone buried himself in his own affairs as if there were no end to this life . . . even when everything teetered on the edge of the abyss."

54. Roth, "Talk with Aharon Appelfeld," 30.

55. One of the strengths of recent studies like Christopher Browning's *Ordinary Men: Reserve Police Battalion 101 and the Final Solution in Poland* (New York: Harper Collins, 1992) and *The Path to Genocide: Essays on Launching the Final Solution* (New York: Cambridge University Press, 1992) is how clearly they show the crucial role of individual decisions and choices in carrying out the genocide.

4. BACKSHADOWING AND THE RHETORIC
OF VICTIMIZATION

1. Aharon Appelfeld, *The Immortal Bartfuss,* trans. Jeffrey M. Green (New York: Harper and Row, 1989), 107. The depiction of the money-grubbing, petty Jews in this novel succeeds in undermining the Israeli desire for "positive" heroes without succumbing to the same allegorical reductiveness as *Badenheim* because in *Bartfuss,* and in other stories set in contemporary Israel, the Shoah has already occurred and the characters (who often lived through it directly), as well as the author and reader, know about the genocide. Consequently, the Shoah cannot serve as a privileged focus of knowledge by which we can judge the characters and their actions without anyone in the book being aware of the terms and criteria of judgment. In *Bartfuss,* the Shoah does not function as a guarantor of authoritative judgment precisely because of its availability to and presence in everyone's consciousness.

2. Alan Mintz, *Hurban: Responses to Catastrophe in Hebrew Literature* (New York: Columbia University Press, 1984), 227–28.

3. Ibid., 228. A basically optimistic assessment of the ideals and accomplishments of novelists whose work was composed within the "Palmah" ethos is found in Gershon Shaked, *The Shadows Within: Essays on Modern Jewish Writers* (Philadelphia: Jewish Publication Society, 1987), 145: "The earliest Hebrew writers in Eretz Israel—the majority of them native-born, or 'sabras'—were the first children of a culture in formation. Born in the 1920s and raised on a Hebrew vernacular and a Hebrew literary tradition, they built upon the foundations for a new society that had been laid by their parents. Most of these young writers identified with the ideals of the parent generation—the pioneering elite of the Labor movement. . . . Not without reason were they called the '1948 generation' or the 'Palmah generation,' after the vanguard brigade of the Jewish armed forces during the 1940s. The 1948 generation was educated to fulfill the pioneer ethos of their parents— most were educated according to a curriculum that broke completely with those that had molded the youth of the heder, the yeshiva, and the gymnasium. . . . This tendency was marked by an increasing dissociation from religious traditions and from the social values of the Diaspora . . . [and was marked by an] acute distaste for the image of the 'Diaspora Jew.' " For a more skeptical, and I think more accurate assessment, see Robert Alter, "A World Awry," in *Times Literary Supplement,* May 3, 1985, p. 498: " 'Normalization,' . . . was once an important plank in the Zionist platform: the Jews, after centuries of deformation in the Diaspora were to become *kekhol ha-*

goyim, like all the nations. The Generation of '48 struggled with this ideal and . . . wrote fiction under its aegis. This was above all a fiction about life in peer groups . . . [and] the novelists tended to derive their models of fiction from Hebrew translations of Soviet Socialist realism. . . . Almost all the characters were young, male, native Israelis . . . baffled by their historical predicament rather than by their own neuroses. Fiction was thus imagined out of the center of national life and evinced little interest in anything away from the center."

4. Shaked, *Shadows Within,* 18.

5. Haim Hazaz, "The Sermon," trans. Ben Halpern, *Partisan Review,* no. 23 (Winter 1956): 171–87. The lines quoted are from pages 173–75. The story has been reprinted, with a helpful introduction by the editor, in Robert Alter, ed., *Modern Hebrew Literature* (West Orange, N.J.: Behrman House, 1975), 253–87.

6. Hazaz, "The Sermon," 183. See, however, Sidra DeKoven Ezrahi's ingenious but implausibly affirmative reading of "The Sermon": "This story, written in 1942, can be viewed as a proximate and radical response to catastrophe. What is being put forward here is a daring proposal for *non-Apocalyptic closure.*" Ezrahi, "Considering the Apocalypse: Is the Writing on the Wall Only Graffiti?" in Berel Lang, ed., *Writing and the Holocaust* (New York: Holmes and Meier, 1988), 145–46. Yosef Hayim Yerushalmi's *Zakhor: Jewish History and Jewish Memory* (Seattle: University of Washington Press, 1982), 97, quotes from "The Sermon" to illustrate a somewhat different argument from the one at issue here, but its interpretation of the story is much closer to my reading than to Ezrahi's. For an explicit critique of Yudke's view of Jewish history, see Benjamin Harshav, *Language in Time of Revolution* (Berkeley and Los Angeles: University of California Press, 1993), 7–8. The larger historical questions that Yudka's speech so simplifies are persuasively analyzed in David Biale's fine study, *Power and Powerlessness in Jewish History* (New York: Schocken, 1986).

7. Gershom Scholem, "With Gershom Scholem: An Interview," in Werner J. Dannhauser, ed. and trans., *On Jews and Judaism in Crisis* (New York: Schocken, 1976), 40–41.

8. Emil Fackenheim, *The Jewish Return into History: Reflections in the Age of Auschwitz and a New Jerusalem* (New York: Schocken, 1978).

9. Jonathan Boyarin, *Storm from Paradise: The Politics of Jewish Memory* (Minneapolis: University of Minnesota Press, 1992), 125.

10. Gershom Scholem, "Israel and the Diaspora," in Dannhauser, ed., *On Jews and Judaism in Crisis,* 248.

11. Shabtai Teveth, *Ben-Gurion: The Burning Ground, 1886–1948* (Boston: Houghton Mifflin, 1987), 539.

12. This sentence is quoted in *The New York Times,* April 3, 1992, p. A9. The prevalence of such a view cannot, however, be attributed purely to the Israeli right-wing parties. In the Knesset, Menahem Begin liked to point out that Abba Eban, the liberal ambassador to the United Nations (1948–49) and to the United States (1950–59), later a minister of education and culture (1960–63) and foreign minister (1966–74), had also described the pre-1967 borders as "Auschwitz lines." Quoted in Tom Segev, *The Seventh Million: The Israelis and the Holocaust,* trans. Haim Watzman (New York: Hill and Wang, 1993), 393.

It is worth pointing out, however, that increasingly there are encouraging signs suggesting that Israeli political debates are moving beyond a rhetoric of self-justifying *ressentiment.* For example, during the Knesset debates on how to help the Muslims being slaughtered in the "ethnic cleansing" in the former Yugoslav republics, the memory of the Shoah was regularly invoked, not out of self-interest but as a reason to assist strangers of a different faith and historical/ethnic allegiance. Quoted in *The New York Times,* August 9, 1992, p. Y11.

13. The text of the letters exchanged between Rabin and Arafat are printed in *The New York Times,* September 10, 1993, p. A8.

14. I have taken Yaron Ezrahi's description from an article by Thomas Friedman, "The Brave New Middle East," *The New York Times,* September 10, 1993, pp. A1, A10.

15. On the history of the agonizing debates raised by these questions among Zionist thinkers, see especially, Anita Shapira, *Land and Power: The Zionist Resort to Force, 1881–1948,* trans. William Templer (New York: Oxford University Press, 1992).

16. Walter Benjamin, "The Task of the Translator," in *Illuminations,* ed. Hannah Arendt, trans. Harry Zohn (New York: Schocken, 1969), 70.

17. Aharon Appelfeld, *The Retreat,* trans. Dalya Bilu (New York: Penguin, 1985), 62, 74. All further references are to this edition and are to be acknowledged in the body of the text.

18. Segev, *Seventh Million,* 109. The very term *yishuv,* as Benjamin Harshav rightly notes, is "a loaded word, meaning 'a stable settlement,' as opposed to the 'Exile' of the 'Wandering Jew.' " Harshav, *Language in Time of Revolution,* x.

19. Berel Lang, *Act and Idea in the Nazi Genocide* (Chicago: University of Chicago Press, 1990), 212n5.

20. Yael Feldman offers just such an interpretation of Appelfeld's thus far untranslated novel, *Michvat Ha'or* (Searing Light) published in 1980. According to Feldman, "this whole novel in fact reads like a ferocious parody of the Zionist enterprise of re-education, of the attempt to 'baptize' the survivors as 'new Jews.' . . . At certain moments the distinction between Zionist and Nazi rhetoric is blurred (as in the repetition of the phrase 'Work is good. Work purifies' . . . or in the constant talk about the survivors' deformities and blemishes [*moomim, pegamin*] that need 'correction.')" For Feldman, though, "*Searing Light* stands alone in his [Appelfeld's] oeuvre," and she adds the fascinating detail that "rumor has it that the author forbade any translation of this work." Feldman, "Whose Story Is It Anyway: Ideology and Psychology in the Representation of the Shoah in Israeli Literature," in Saul Friedlander, ed., *Probing the Limits of Representation: Nazism and the "Final Solution"* (Cambridge: Harvard University Press, 1992), 232–34. But if my reading of *Badenheim 1939* and *The Retreat* is valid, then the same uncanny parallelism between Zionist and Nazi rhetoric that dominates *Searing Light* governs Appelfeld's earlier books about prewar European Jewry as well. I suspect that because *Searing Light* deals with survivors, whereas the characters in *Badenheim 1939* and *The Retreat* presumably will all be murdered in the Shoah, it has been easier for critics to recognize, and for the novelist to acknowledge, the bitterness of the book's perspective on Israeli attitudes. But what is intended as a *critique* of Zionist contempt in a text set in Israel is actually the only judgment voiced and given implicit authorial sanction in the novels set in the final days of Austro-German Jewish existence. Appelfeld simultaneously accepts (in his "European" novels) and indicts (in his "Israeli" books) a particularly harsh Zionist interpretation of the psychological and moral worthiness of the European Diaspora, and he does so without ever confronting that central contradiction in his thinking. It is as though he has internalized the very attitudes he wants to contest, because he sees them as the *only* terms by which to understand the culture that perished in the Shoah.

21. Gary Saul Morson, *The Boundaries of Genre: Dostoevsky's "Diary of a Writer" and the Traditions of Literary Utopia* (Austin: University of Texas Press, 1981), 118.

22. Meir Shalev, *The Blue Mountain,* trans. Hillel Halkin (New York: Harper and Row, 1991), 226.

23. I say "probably" deliberately because, at his best, Appelfeld is a very canny writer, and his relationship to the rhetoric and ideology of left-Zionism is sufficiently embattled to make it just conceivable that the parallelisms

I have mentioned also figured in his own awareness while he was writing *The Retreat.* But if this is so, he has been extremely careful to cover his traces, and none of the reviews that I have read interpret the novel as anything other than a critique of Austro-Jewish self-hatred in the period just before the Shoah.

24. The term "semiotic totalitarian" was coined by Gary Saul Morson in *Hidden in Plain View: Narrative and Creative Potentials in "War and Peace"* (Stanford: Stanford University Press, 1987).

25. Yosef Hayim Yerushalmi, *Zakhor: Jewish History and Jewish Memory* (Seattle: University of Washington Press, 1982), 98.

26. There are too many well-known instances of this phenomenon for me to make any example truly representative. But the American-born painter R. B. Kitaj's *First Diasporist Manifesto* (London: Thames and Hudson, 1989) can serve as an instructive instance of the most common tendencies. Kitaj, born in 1932, has become increasingly aware of his Jewishness but sees it almost exclusively as defined by the Shoah. Kitaj regards himself as a kind of "survivor" who identifies with "menaced Jewry," and links the alienation of modern artists to the fate of the Jews. Similar identifications, although formulated with more subtlety, have marked some of the most impassioned texts by writers like Susan Sontag and George Steiner. Finally, at the extreme of self-aggrandizement, there is a volume like the Canadian poet Irving Layton's *Fortunate Exile* (Toronto: McClelland and Stuart, 1987), in which "the Jews' unique and tragic encounter with history" serves largely to validate the author's claims for his own historical importance. I discuss Layton's collection from this perspective in "Usurpations: A Poetics of Catastrophe and the Language of Jewish History," *TriQuarterly,* no. 79 (Fall 1990): 207–19.

27. David Evanier, "Invisible Man: The Lynching of Yankel Rosenbaum" *New Republic,* October 14, 1991, pp. 21–22.

28. *Kristallnacht* was ably defined by one letter writer to *The New York Times,* who had witnessed it directly, as the beginning of "the physical and institutional destruction of the Jewish community by the political power of the state." The writer goes on to say that "however ugly were the anti-Semitic slogans and the assaultive behavior of people in the streets [during the Crown Heights riots] . . . one thing that clearly did not take place was a Kristallnacht." Letter by Henry Schwarzschild, *New York Times,* October 5, 1991, p. A18.

29. Similarly, on October 29, 1992, when seventeen-year-old Lemrick Nelson, Jr., was acquitted of all charges in the murder of Rosenbaum, the Hasidic and black communities were united in the conviction that the whole trial was determined by racist motives. But for the one group, Nelson's initial

arrest and trial was the result of collusion between a corrupt police force and a suborned city medical examiner's office eager to find a "black sacrificial lamb"; for the second group, the teenager's release was seen as due largely to the jury's anti-Semitism and fear of mob violence. An official report of the Crown Heights episode, commissioned by New York Governor Mario Cuomo and overseen by Richard Girgenti, the state's Director of Criminal Justice, concluded that the entire city administration, including the Mayor David Dinkins, Police Commissioner Lee P. Brown, and top police commanders, were all at fault for not preventing the escalation of violence. The report also blamed Nelson's complete acquittal on inept police procedure in handling the evidence against him, and prejudicial "statements and demeanor" by the presiding judge, New York Supreme Court Justice Edward Rappaport. Racism, the report concluded, was not a major issue in the jury's verdict. *New York Times,* July 21, 1993, pp. A1, B10.

30. For a history and internal logic of the theme of the victim-turned-oppressor, see Michael André Bernstein, *Bitter Carnival: Ressentiment and the Abject Hero* (Princeton: Princeton University Press, 1992).

31. A. B. Yehoshua, *Between Right and Right,* trans. A. Schwartz (Garden City, N.Y.: Doubleday, 1981), 17.

32. For example, an anonymous African American senior at the University of California, Berkeley, told the local campus newspaper that he had participated in the April–May 1992 riots that followed the acquittal of the four Los Angeles police officers in the Rodney King beating case. He "confessed to beating up innocent white bystanders after the King verdict was announced. 'I admit I've beaten up so-called "innocent" white people this weekend—[they've] never owned slaves, but [they're] reaping the benefits of [their] ancestors,' he said. 'I have no guilt,' he added. 'How else can you learn how it feels to have shit done to you just because of the color of your skin?' he asked." Kim Balchios, "Searching for Justice," *Daily Californian,* May 5, 1992, p. 2.

33. *Gush Emunim* (The Block of the Faithful) is among the most powerful of the militant orthodox movements dedicated to expanding Israeli settlements throughout the greater territory of Biblical Israel. One of its official slogans is *af sha'al* (not an inch), which aptly summarizes the group's position on any negotiations involving territorial compromise. Baruch Goldstein's rampage occurred on February 25, 1994, at a mosque in Hebron.

34. Robert Alter, "Deformations of the Holocaust," *Commentary,* February 1981, 49. Emphasis mine.

35. Lawrence L. Langer, *Holocaust Testimonies: The Ruins of Memory* (New Haven: Yale University Press, 1991), 59.

36. Ibid., 204.

37. Primo Levi, *Survival in Auschwitz*, trans. Stuart Woolf (New York: Macmillan, 1961), 79. I have included the original Italian phrasing in order to make clear that Levi does not believe that the world of the Lager unmasks fundamental human traits, always present but normally kept hidden beneath a fragile layer of quotidian civility. Levi, *Se questo è un uomo*, in *Opere* 1 (Turin: Einaudi, 1987), 88.

38. Sylvia Plath, "Daddy," in *The Collected Poems of Sylvia Plath* (New York: Harper and Row, 1981), 223. It is, no doubt, only fair to point out that a different reading of the poem would emphasize its rhetoric as the re-creation of a child's distorted vision—the language of a child who grew up in America during the war and internalized American propaganda images. But such a reading, defended to me most forcefully by my colleague, Alex Zwerdling, still seems to me ultimately unpersuasive.

39. Joseph Conrad, *Lord Jim*, ed. Thomas C. Moser (New York: Norton Critical Editions, 1968), 197, 130–31.

40. Ezrahi, "Considering the Apocalypse," 149.

41. Lang, *Act and Idea in the Nazi Genocide*, 65.

42. Caryl Emerson, "Bakhtin and Women: A Non-Topic with Immense Publications," an unpublished paper the author generously showed me in manuscript.

43. Michael Frayn, *Constructions* (London: Wildwood House, 1974), no. 205, no pagination.

44. Michael R. Marrus, "The Use and Misuse of the Holocaust," in Peter Hayes, ed., *Lessons and Legacies: The Meaning of the Holocaust in a Changing World* (Evanston, Ill.: Northwestern University Press, 1991), 116.

45. Frayn, *Constructions*, no. 26.

5. SIDESHADOWING AND THE PRINCIPLE OF THE INSUFFICIENT CAUSE

1. Austria declared war on Serbia on July 28, 1914, and on Russia on August 6; the British and French responded by declaring war on Austria on August 12. Other combatants continued to join in the conflict at later dates, as, for example, the Belgians, who waited until August 28.

2. The Collateral Campaign (*Parallelaktion*) is entirely Musil's own invention and serves as a wonderfully comic device that allows the novel to examine the leading political, social, artistic, and intellectual currents of pre-

war Austria by letting them compete for dominance in the campaign's search for a national slogan.

3. Victoria Yablonsky, "Ambiguous Visions: Ulrich's Inner States in *Der Mann ohne Eigenschaften*," Ph.D. diss., Columbia University, 1985, p. 32.

4. "Also ich bin überzeugt, daß fast jeder Mensch heute unser Zeitalter für das geordnetste hält, was es je gegeben hat . . . daß der Geist der Neuzeit eben in dieser größeren Ordnung liegt und daß die Reiche von Ninive und Rom an irgendeiner Schlamperei zugrunde gegangen sein müssen. Ich glaube die meisten Menschen empfinden so und setzen stillschweigend voraus, daß die Vergangenheit zur Strafe vergangen ist, für irgendetwas, das nicht in Ordnung war."

5. "Nichts ist in der Diplomatie so gefährlich wie das unsachliche Reden vom Frieden! Jedesmal, wenn das Bedürfnis danach eine gewisse Höhe erreicht hat und nicht mehr zu halten war, ist noch ein Krieg daraus entstanden!"

6. "Es hatte damals gerade eine neue Zeit begonnen (denn das tut sie in jedem Augenblick). . . . Es war eine bewegte Zeit, die um Ende 1913 und Anfang 1914. Aber auch die Zeit zwei oder fünf Jahre vorher war eine bewegte Zeit gewesen."

7. Joseph Roth's *Radetzkymarsch* (1932) is probably the best-known Austrian novel that deals with the collapse of the Habsburg Empire. Unlike Musil, Roth foreshadows the war at every opportunity, usually in an extraordinarily overwrought rhetoric. For example, at the regimental summer fête that takes place almost at the novel's end, a messenger arrives to interrupt the dancing with news from headquarters. The atmosphere, predictably enough, is tense with the electricity of a summer storm, and the horseman's approach is described as taking place amid "flickering white sheet-lightning and darkened by purple clouds" (umflackert von weißen Blitzen und von violetten Wolken umdüstert). As the Colonel tears open the message, the footman "could not control his suddenly trembling hand" (konnte dennoch nicht seine plötzlich zitternde Hand beherrschen). The news, of course, is the report of Franz Ferdinand's assassination, and in the footman's mind there is a "supernatural connection" (übernatürlicher Zusammenhang) between the thunder and lightening breaking out all around him and the dreadful news from Sarajevo. Roth, *Radetzkymarsch* (Berlin: Gustav Kiepenheuer, 1932), 512–14. The enormous critical as well as popular success of the book is evidence of how deeply wedded readers are to the conventions of fore- and backshadowing that Musil is deliberately seeking to undo.

8. "Größenteils entsteht Geschichte aber ohne Autoren. Sie entsteht

nicht von einem Zentrum her, sondern von der Peripherie. Aus kleinen Ursachen. . . . Der Weg der Geschichte ist also nicht der eines Billardballs, der, einmal abgestoßen, eine bestimmte Bahn durchläuft, sondern er ähnelt dem Weg der Wolken, ähnelt dem Weg eines durch die Gassen Streichenden, der hier von einem Schatten, dort von einer Menschengruppe oder einer seltsamen Verschneidung von Häuserfronten abgelenkt wird und schließlich an eine Stelle gerät, die er weder gekannt hat, noch erreichen wollte.''

9. '' 'Wissen Sie, daß ich vom Kopf bis zum Fuß erschauere, wenn ich ihn sehe? Er erinnert mich an den Tod!' 'Ein ungewöhnlich lebensfreundlich aussehender Tod. . . .' 'Aber mich ergreift eine Panik, wenn er mich anspricht . . . Mich beschleicht eine unbeschreibliche, unbegreifliche, traumhafte Angst!' ''

10. Wolfdietrich Rasch sees the juxtapositioning of characters, plot motifs, and ideas as central to Musil's compositional technique. See Rasch, *Über Robert Musils Roman Der Mann ohne Eigenschaften* (Göttingen: Vandenhoeck and Ruprecht, 1967) and his essay "Musil: 'Der Mann ohne Eigenschaften,' " in Benno von Wiese, ed., *Der deutsche Roman: Vom Barok bis zur Gegenwart* (Düsseldorf: A. Bagel, 1963), 2:361–419. Götz Müller's *Ideologiekritik und Metasprache in Robert Musils Roman 'Der Mann ohne Eigenschaften'* (Munich: W. Fink, 1972) usefully analyzes how Musil's juxtaposing various discourses discredits characters like Arnheim or Leinsdorf who use ideas for self-assertive and ideologically tendentious reasons. Philip Payne also comments on Musil's "provocative juxtaposing of material. (A chapter which explores the inner world of Arnheim, for example, is followed by one which recreates the mood of Moosebrugger in his prison cell)." Payne, *Robert Musil's "The Man Without Qualities": A Critical Study* (Cambridge: Cambridge University Press, 1988), 101.

11. For a description of how Graf Leinsdorf and Diotima conceive of the membership of the Collatoral Campaign, see chapter 24, pp. 98–103; 1:139–44. Wilkins and Kaiser needlessly reverse Graf Leinsdorf's word order and translate the catch-phrase as "culture and capital," wherever it occurs in the novel. Their decision distorts the hierarchy of values made evident in the German wording.

12. "Denn wenn diese Art Leute im Deutschen Reich auch noch nicht obenauf waren . . . [ein Gerücht flüstert daß] dieser Sohn . . . sich auf eine Reichministerschaft vorbereitete. Nach der Meinung des Sektionschefs Tuzzi war dies freilich ganz und gar ausgeschlossen, außer es ginge ein Weltuntergang voran.'' (For although people of this sort were not yet quite on

top in the German empire . . . this son . . . was preparing to take on a position as a minister of the Reich. In Permanent Secretary Tuzzi's opinion this was of course utterly out of the question, unless preceded by a world cataclysm.) (96; 1:136)

13. Hannah Hickman, *Robert Musil and the Culture of Vienna* (London: Croom Helm, 1984), 133.

14. "Er kämpfte um seine Seligkeit."

15. "Ein Jahr Urlaub von seinem Leben."

16. "Einen . . . bewußten Utopismus."

17. "Etwas . . . daß man Möglichkeitssinn nennen kann. . . . Ein mögliches Erlebnis oder eine mögliche Wahrheit sind nicht gleich wirklichem Erlebnis und wirklicher Wahrheit weniger dem Werte des Wirklichseins."

18. Among the classic critiques of the utopian impulse along these lines are Edmund Burke's *Reflections on the Revolution in France,* and both the journalism and the fiction of Fyodor Dostoevsky, especially *The Possessed* and *The Diary of A Writer.* Valuable discussions can also be found in Karl Popper, *The Open Society and Its Enemies,* 2 vols. (London: Routledge, 5th rev. ed., 1966) and *The Poverty of Historicism* (London: Routledge, corrected ed., 1961); Friedrich von Hayek, *The Road to Serfdom* (London: Routledge, 1944); Norman Cohn, *The Pursuit of the Millennium* (London: Secker and Warburg, 1957); Leo Strauss, *On Tyranny: Including the Strauss-Kojève Correspondence,* ed. Victor Gourevitch and Michael Roth (New York: Free Press, 1993); Hannah Arendt, *The Origins of Totalitarianism* (New York: Harcourt, Brace, 1951) and *On Revolution* (New York: Viking, 1963); Isaiah Berlin, *Against the Current* (New York: Viking, 1980) and *The Crooked Timber of Humanity* (New York: Knopf, 1991); Jacob Talmon, *The Origins of Totalitarian Democracy* (London: Secker and Warburg, 1952) and *Political Messianism: The Romantic Phase* (London: Secker and Warburg, 1960); Sylvia L. Thrupp, ed., *Millennial Dreams in Action* (New York: Schocken, 1970); Melvin J. Lasky, *Utopia and Revolution* (Chicago: University of Chicago Press, 1976); Gary Saul Morson, *The Boundaries of Genre: Dostoevsky's Diary of a Writer and the Traditions of Literary Utopia* (Austin: University of Texas Press, 1981) and *Hidden in Plain View: Narrative and Creative Potentials in "War and Peace"* (Stanford: Stanford University Press, 1987); Bernard Yack, *The Longing for Total Revolution: Philosophical Sources of Social Discontent from Rousseau to Marx and Nietzsche* (Princeton: Princeton University Press, 1986).

19. I offer a detailed analysis of how just such a certainty led one noted writer, Ezra Pound, to embrace Italian fascism in *The Tale of the Tribe: Ezra Pound and the Modern Verse Epic* (Princeton: Princeton University Press, 1980).

20. For an interesting discussion of the link between parodic and utopian thinking in three of the century's most important German novelists, see Manfred Sera's *Utopie und Parodie bei Musil, Broch und Thomas Mann* (Bonn: H. Bouvier, 1969).

21. "Daß wahrscheinlich auch Gott von seiner Welt am liebsten im Conjunctivus potentialis spreche . . . denn Gott macht die Welt und denkt dabei, es könnte ebensogut anders sein."

22. The study of Musil's *Nachlaß* has become both one of the most contentious and specialized areas of Musil scholarship. Useful contributions to the debates about the status of the *Nachlaß* include Uwe Baur and Elisabeth Castex, *Robert Musil: Untersuchungen* (Königstein, Taunus: Athenaum, 1980); Wilhelm Bausinger, *Studien zu einer historisch-kritischen Ausgabe von Robert Musils Roman "Der Mann ohne Eigenschaften"* (Reinbek bei Hamburg: Rowohlt, 1964); Elisabeth Castex, "Probleme und Ziele der Forschung am Nachlaß Robert Musils," *Colloquia Germanica* 10 (1976–77): 267–79; Wolfgang Freese, ed., *Philologie und Kritik* (Munich: W. Fink, 1981); Adolf Frisé, "Unvollendet-unvollendbar? Überlegungen zum Torso des 'Mann ohne Eigenschaften,' " *Musil-Forum* 6 (1980): 79–104; Wolfdietrich Rasch, *Über Robert Musils Roman Der Mann ohne Eigenschaften* (Göttingen: Vandenhoeck and Ruprecht, 1967); Marie-Louise Roth, Renate Schröder-Werle, and Hans Zeller, eds., *Nachla- und Editionsprobleme bei modernen Schriftstellern: Beiträge zu den Internationalen Robert Musil Symposien* (Bern; Las Vegas, 1981); Eithne Wilkins, "Musils unvollendeter Roman 'Die Zwillingsschwester,' " in *Colloquia Germanica* 10 (1976–77): 220–36; Hans Zeller, "Vitium aut virtus? Philologisches zu Adolf Frisés Musilausgaben, mit prinzipiellen Überlegungen zur Frage des Texteingriffs," in the special number *Probleme neugermanistischer Edition* of the *Zeitschrift für deutsche Philologie* 101 (1982): 210–44. Although a new translation of *Der Mann ohne Eigenschaften,* including some of the *Nachlaß,* has been announced several times during the past few years, so far it has not yet appeared in print. Consequently, English-speaking readers have had to rely entirely on second-hand accounts of Musil's posthumous drafts and fragments. Although I am far from being an expert in the technical issues concerning the *Nachlaß,* my general sense concurs with Philip Payne's that "for all their quarrels over the *Nachlass* . . . scholars agree on one point: no definitive final version of the novel can be established however hard one combs through all that Musil wrote." Payne, *Robert Musil's "The Man Without Qualities,"* 57. One implication of this situation, however, has tended to go unremarked: because there is no one, agreed-on ending, *all* of Musil's different suggestions and outlines can be read as sideshadows of one another—like

the intellectual debates of the published sections, the possible paths sketched out in the *Nachlaß* are choices that exist only as sideshadows of a never realized, because humanly and logically unrealizable, closure.

23. Hence, the apparent "solutions" and "transcendences" that seem to be attained by Ulrich and Agathe in their conversations break down as soon as they return to ordinary society and confront the counter-pressures of quotidian living. The structural function of Agathe's forging a will is to motivate the plot to drag them back, in the most demeaning way possible, into the daily world, as Hagauer's legal responses make Ulrich and Agathe consult lawyers, worry about a possible trial, etc. But as a motivating device, the forged will is unnecessarily melodramatic. Far more effective is the simple, low-key way the "fall" from their insights and intimacies is narrated at the end of one of Diotima's parties: Agathe is tired, somewhat bored and wants to go home—Ulrich would like to join her, but as various guests keep interrupting his departure to talk to him, he finds himself constrained by the social world not to leave, and so Agathe, disappointed in him, returns home alone, while he is dissatisfied with her for leaving early and without him. The world of Viennese social life by itself already acts as a "test" of their intimacy and shows its inadequacy as a real solution. These chapters experiment with what one can call the "problem of the morning after a transcendent experience." Musil's question is: what has that experience and its attendant insights transformed in real, everyday life?

24. For two interesting discussions related to this theme, see Marike Finlay, *The Potential of Modern Discourse: Musil, Pierce, and Perturbation* (Bloomington: Indiana University Press, 1990), and Thomas Harrison, *Essayism: Conrad, Musil and Pirandello* (Baltimore: Johns Hopkins University Press, 1992). Harrison's study has a number of strengths, but, given its focus, its relative neglect of Montaigne is especially surprising. I have also benefited from a particularly insightful essay relating Montaigne, Musil, and Svevo by Dalya M. Sachs, a graduate student at U.C. Berkeley in a seminar I taught on sideshadowing.

25. "Millionen Toter eines erschütternden Kriegs."

26. "Was Hagauer später Vorschubleistung nannte"; "Trotzdem war es wie ein kleiner Riß im Schleier des Lebens, durch den das teilnahmslose Nichts schaut, und es wurde damals der Grund zu manchem gelegt, was später geschah"; "Das bedeutete also nichts weniger, als daß Agathe schon in dieser Zeit die Absicht gehabt hätte, sich zu töten."

27. "In dieser Zeit, da der Schutt 'des vergeblich Gefühlten,' den ein Zeitalter über dem anderen hinterläßt, Bergeshöhe erreicht hat, ohne daß

etwas dagegen geschähe. Das Kriegsministerium darf also beruhigt dem nächsten Massenunglück entgegensehen. Ulrich sagte das Schicksal vorher und hatte davon keine Ahnung.''

28. See Leo Bersani, '' 'The Culture of Redemption': Marcel Proust and Melanie Klein,'' *Critical Inquiry,* vol. 12, no. 2 (Winter 1986): 402, 404: ''I speak of an ambiguity which has led some of Proust's readers to raise the extremely peculiar question of whether or not the text we have is the one which the narrator tells us, at the end of *Le temps retrouvé,* that he finally set out to write. . . . *À la recherche du temps perdu* is a nonattributable autobiographical novel. The experience it records may, it is suggested, belong to Marcel Proust, or it may belong to a fictional character named Marcel, or it may belong to a fictional character not named Marcel. Or, finally, it may belong to no one at all.'' The essay is reprinted as ''Death and Literary Authority: Marcel Proust and Melanie Klein,'' in Bersani, *The Culture of Redemption* (Cambridge: Harvard University Press, 1990), 7–28.

29. ''Der Typus einer Vernunft . . . die aber solche [Erkenntnisse] zu finden und zu systematisieren strebte, welche dem Gefühl neue und kühne Richtungen gäben, auch wenn sie selbst vielleicht nur bloße Plausibilitäten blieben, eine Vernunft also, für die das Denken nur dazu da wäre, um irgendwelchen noch ungewissen Weisen Mensch zu sein ein intellektuelles Stützgerüst zu geben.'' From the 1912 essay ''Das Geistliche, der Modernismus und die Metaphysik,'' in *Prosa und Stücke, Kleine Prosa, Aphorismen, Autobiographisches, Essays und Reden, Kritik,* ed. Adolf Frisé, (Reinbek bei Hamburg: Rowohlt, 1978), 989. The essay has been translated as ''The Religious Spirit, Modernism, and Metaphysics,'' in Burton Pike and David S. Luft, eds. and trans., *Precision and Soul: Essays and Addresses* (Chicago: University of Chicago Press, 1990), 21–25. I have amended the translation in several places.

30. For a fascinating recent exploration of some of the same issues told from the perspectives of a female protagonist, see Carol Anshaw, *Aquamarine* (New York: Houghton Mifflin, 1992). The novel opens with a brief prologue set at the 1968 Mexico City Olympics during the women's 100-meter freestyle swim competition. We watch seventeen-year-old Jesse Austin lose the gold medal to her rival, and lover of one night, Marty Finch. In the following sections, each dated July 1990, three equally possible and richly described future versions of Jesse Austin are depicted. In one, she has gone back to her small Missouri hometown and settled into an affectionate but not very stirring marriage, a budding career as a real estate agent, and a not-quite consummated affair with a local skywriter. In the next, she is a lesbian lit-

erature professor in New York, visiting her Missouri home in the company of her lover, a glamorous television soap opera actress. In the third version, Jesse lives in a seedy Florida beach town, running a failing swim school and trying to cope with little money, two difficult teenage children, a maddeningly self-satisfied ex-husband, and a friendly but not deeply committed black lover. Many of the same characters appear in each section, as do numerous aspects of Jesse's own temperament, and Anshaw manages to make each future convincing as one of the paths Jesse might have taken after Mexico. By bestowing the narrative attention and energy equally to each of the imagined destinies, the novel makes certain we read each of Jesse's counterlives in the light of the other possibilities, and each event is sideshadowed by the whole dense swarm of parallel circumstances, actions, and thoughts that have been traced in the course of *Aquamarine*'s unfolding.

31. Louis Begley, *The Man Who Was Late* (New York: Knopf, 1993), 199.

32. "Im Grunde wissen in den Jahren der Lebensmitte wenig Menschen mehr, wie sie eigentlich zu sich selbst gekommen sind, zu ihren Vergnügungen, ihrer Weltanschauung, ihrer Frau, ihrem Charakter, Beruf und ihren Erfolgen, aber sie haben das Gefühl, daß sich nun nicht mehr viel ändern kann. Es ließ sich sogar behaupten, daß sie betrogen worden seien, denn man kann nirgends einen zureichenden Grund dafür entdecken, daß alles gerade so kam, wie es gekommen ist; es hätte auch anders kommen können."

33. Cynthia Ozick, "Alfred Chester's Wig," *The New Yorker,* March 30, 1992, p. 80.

34. "Parce que je n'accompagnai pas mon père à un dîner officiel où il devait y avoir les Bontemps avec leur nièce Albertine, petite jeune fille presque encore enfant." Marcel Proust, "À l'ombre des jeunes filles en fleurs," in *À la recherche du temps perdu* (Paris: Bibliothèque de la Pléiade, 1987), 1:615. Earlier in the same volume, Gilberte briefly describes Albertine herself as "la fameuse 'Albertine.' Elle sera sûrement très 'fast' " (503), and although this incident holds a similar pleasure for the re-reader as the one I have quoted, it is less intense because Marcel is not directly involved and there is no suggestion that he might have become interested in Albertine much sooner.

35. In one of the many moments of deep-rooted affinity that resonate between *À la recherche du temps perdu* and *The Man Without Qualities,* Musil's narrator uses a similar image of the beloved being transformed from one figure amid a circle of friends into the lover's unique object of desire: "They [ideas] flash upon the mind in a startling way reminiscent of another sudden

recognition—that of the beloved who has been merely one girl among the other girls till the moment when the lover is suddenly amazed that he could ever have supposed any of the others to be her equal.'' (Daß ihr überraschendes Aufleuchten an das der Geliebten erinnert, die längst schon zwischen den anderen Freundinnen da war, ehe der bestürzte Freier zu verstehen aufhört, daß er ihr andere hat gleichstellen können.) (719–20; 3:74–75). The same passage also offers an amusing index of the difference between the two novels, since in Musil the image is used not only as a comment on the nature of desire but, more important, on the accidental and unexpected ways one often comes upon a decisive idea when working on a particularly intractable problem in mathematics!

36. ''Peut-être parce qu'elle était ennuyeuse, ou parce qu'elle était méchante, ou parce qu'elle était d'une branche inférieure, ou peut-être sans aucune raisonne.'' Proust, *À la recherche du temps perdu* 1:323. For an interesting discussion relating this and similar passages in the *Recherche* to the question of ''a demonstration of the failure of hypotheses,'' see Margaret E. Gray, *Postmodern Proust* (Philadelphia: University of Pennsylvania Press, 1992), 56–65.

37. James E. Young, *Writing and Rewriting the Holocaust: Narrative Consequences of Interpretation* (Bloomington: Indiana University Press, 1988), 30. Young is speaking here of the difference between the testimony of a diarist and that of a survivor-memoirist of the Shoah. But his description accurately distinguishes between any retrospective account and one written at the time that the events narrated were taking place, whether those events were catastrophes or not.

38. In these comments I am, of course, not seeking to minimize the role of politics and social history in *À la recherche du temps perdu,* since events like the Dreyfus case and the First World War are both clearly integral to the narrative. But it is nonetheless true that the protagonist is only indirectly caught up in these public crises. Neither event is decisive in shaping Marcel's consciousness, and they cannot be said either to constitute Marcel's most significant experiences or to precipitate the narrator's acutest speculations.

6. (IN PLACE OF A) CONCLUSION

1. The notion of ''prosaics'' in this sense was first made explicit by Gary Saul Morson in *Hidden in Plain View: Narrative and Creative Potentials in "War and Peace"* (Stanford: Stanford University Press, 1987) and in his ''Prosaics:

An Approach to the Humanities," *American Scholar,* Autumn 1988, pp. 515–28. It was further developed by Caryl Emerson and Gary Saul Morson in *Bakhtin: Creation of a Prosaics* (Stanford: Stanford University Press, 1990). I have both drawn upon and questioned Emerson's and Morson's Bakhtin-inspired understanding of prosaics, and suggested other directions and issues that prosaic studies ought to explore in *Bitter Carnival: Ressentiment and the Abject Hero* (Princeton: Princeton University Press, 1992).

2. Ludwig Wittgenstein, *The Blue and Brown Books* (New York: Harper Colophon Books, 1965), 17–19.

3. "Es gibt kein ethisches Handeln, sondern nur einen ethischen Zustand," in *Prosa und Stücke, Kleine Prosa, Aphorismen, Autobiographisches, Essays und Reden, Kritik,* ed. Adolf Frisé (Reinbek bei Hamburg: Rowohlt, 1978), 1017. For a suggestive, but unfortunately rather sketchy discussion of some of the links between Wittgenstein's and Musil's thinking, see Allan Janik and Stephen Toulmin, *Wittgenstein's Vienna* (New York: Simon and Schuster, 1973).

4. I am indebted here to a stimulating letter from Kenneth A. Bruffee in which he raises a series of important questions about my earlier account of prosaic ethics in *Bitter Carnival: Ressentiment and the Abject Hero* (Princeton: Princeton University Press, 1992). See also Bruffee's analysis in *Elegiac Romance: Cultural Change and Loss of the Hero in Modern Fiction* (Ithaca: Cornell University Press, 1983). My discussion in this chapter deliberately returns to some of the formulations I first ventured in *Bitter Carnival,* but augments and, I hope, clarifies them further in light of the new context opened up by the theory of sideshadowing and the concrete example of Jewish history.

5. Amos Funkenstein, "Theological Responses to the Holocaust," in his *Perceptions of Jewish History* (Berkeley and Los Angeles: University of California Press, 1993), 306–37.

6. I have taken these sentences from pages 332–33 of Funkenstein, "Theological Responses to the Holocaust."

7. Walter Benjamin, "The Storyteller," in *Illuminations,* ed. Hannah Arendt, trans. Harry Zohn (New York: Schocken, 1969), 87. In tracing one writer's attempt to forge a new, radically idiosyncratic novelistic voice in modern Hebrew, Robert Alter makes a useful distinction between the European novel's traditional focus on the specific individual and that of "the Hebrew literary tradition . . . from the rabbinic period onward through its multiple historical offshoots . . . [which was] inclined to see the individual

as a prototype or spokesman for the collective." Alter, "Fogel and the Forging of a Hebrew Self," *Prooftexts* 13 (1993): 9.

8. I owe this phrase to Douglas Abrams Arava of the University of California Press.

9. Yehuda Amichai, "Tourists," in Chana Bloch and Stephen Mitchell, eds. and trans., *Selected Poetry of Yehuda Amichai* (New York: Harper and Row, 1986), 137–38.

INDEX

The 42nd Parallel (Dos Passos), 110
1919 (Dos Passos), 110
"1946" (Appelfeld), 52, 152–53n49

Adorno, Theodor W., 42–48, 52, 144–45n1
African Americans: Crown Heights episode, 85–86, 158–59nn28,29; Rodney King riots, 159n32
The Age of Wonders (Appelfeld), 150nn36,38, 153n53
Agnon, S. Y., 24, 137n34
Ahad Ha-Am, 144n62
Akhmatova, Anna, 123
Allegory, Appelfeld's, 66–67, 78, 114–15
Almstadtstraße 43 (Attie), xiii
Alter, Robert, xii–xiii, 133n6, 155n5, 169–70n7; on Appelfeld, 58, 149n34; "Deformations of the Holocaust," 88, 159n34; *Necessary Angels,* 136n27; on Zionist normalization, 154–55n3
Alterman, Nathan, 133n6
Améry, Jean, 49
Amichai, Yehuda, 113, 125–26, 149n33; *Not of This Time, Not of This Place,* 5, 111; poetry, 121, 125–27, 170n9
Analytical Philosophy of History (Danto), 25, 135n19, 138nn36,37,39
Anna Karenina (Tolstoy), 88–89
Anschluss, 24, 32–33, 63–66, 69, 137n35, 152n47
Anshaw, Carol, 5, 166–67n30
Anti-Semitism, 10, 22, 23, 118, 151n44; Austrian, 24, 30–33, 35, 37, 63–64, 139–41nn44,45,48, 149–50n36; in Crown Heights episode, 85–86, 158–59nn28,29; Dante and, 50; French, 33; inner, 142n56; Jewish, 37, 66, 72, 78–81, 142–43n56, 158n23; and *Kristallnacht,* 86, 158n28; in Levi's reading, 49; Nuremberg decrees and, 62–63, 64; and victimhood, 76–77. *See also* Shoah
Apocalyptic rhetoric, 125; history, 9–41, 82, 84–85, 91, 119, 120, 126
Appelfeld, Aharon, 53–88, 119, 133n6, 147–53; *The Age of Wonders,* 150nn36,38, 153n53; "art of intima-

tion," 58–59; backshadowing, 61–69, 95, 96; *Badenheim 1939,* 59–72, 79, 81, 102–3, 114, 118, 123, 150–57; "fable" in, 58, 61–62, 67, 102; *The Immortal Bartfuss,* 74, 154n1; *Michvat Ha'or,* 157n20; and Musil (compared), 95, 96, 101, 102–3; "1946," 52, 152–53n49; *The Retreat,* 62, 78–80, 81, 156n17, 157–58nn20,23; *Searing Light,* 157n20; *To the Land of the Cattails,* 58
Aquamarine (Anshaw), 5, 166–67n30
Arab-Jewish relations, 39–40, 76–77, 144n62
Arafat, Yasir, 77, 156n13
Arava, Douglas Abrams, xii, 170n8
Arendt, Hannah, 24, 72, 137n33, 144n59, 156n16, 163n18, 169n7
Aristotle on tragedy, 9–13
Art: film, 19, 52; paintings, 52–53; performance, 47; photographs, xiii, 53; as redemption, 43. *See also* Literature
Aschheim, Steven E., 149n35
Ashbery, John, 5
Ashkenazi Jews, 149n32
Assimilationism: Agnon and, 24; Appelfeld and, 62, 63–67, 70, 72, 78–79, 102, 119, 149n33, 152–53nn46,49; Clare and, 62, 63; Herzl and, 136n29; Ignatieff and, 17; Musil and, 102; and Shoah, 13, 34, 49–50, 62–67, 72, 119, 152n49; Zionist judgment on, 13, 21–22, 62; Zweig and, 62–63
Attie, Shimon, xiii, 53
Auden, W. H., 121
Auerbach, Erich, 129n2
Augustine, Saint, 131n11
Auschwitz: Fackenheim on, 44, 145n3; fictionalized, 54; Israeli borders and, 77, 156n12; survivors' narratives, 12, 46–47, 48, 49–50, 90, 122
Australia, visas for Austrian Jews, 152n48
Austria: anti-Semitism, 24, 30–33, 35, 37, 63–64, 139–41nn44,45,48, 149–50n36; German annexation of (*Anschluss*), 24, 32–33, 63–66, 69, 137n35, 152n47; Habsburg, 18, 24, 35, 96, 104, 137–38n35, 161n7; Musil's Collateral Campaign, 96–98, 100,

171

Compositor:	Impressions, a division of Edwards Brothers
Text:	10.5/14 Baskerville
Display:	Baskerville
Printer:	Edwards Brothers
Binder:	Edwards Brothers